CHICAGO

great ESCAPES

- Weekend Getaways
- Nature Hideaways
- Day Trips
- Easy Planning
- Best Places to Visit

Karla Zimmerman

CHICAGO

The Countryman Press • Woodstock, Vermont

DEDICATION

For Eric, my P.F.L.

We welcome your comments and suggestions. Please contact Editor,
The Countryman Press, P.O. Box 748, Woodstock, Vermont 05091,
or e-mail countrymanpress@wwnorton.com.

ISBN 978-0-88150-844-4

Map by Paul Woodward, © 2009 The Countryman Press
Book design by Bodenweber Design
Text composition by Chelsea Cloeter

Published by The Countryman Press
P.O. Box 748
Woodstock, Vermont 05091

Distributed by W. W. Norton & Company, Inc.
500 Fifth Avenue
New York, NY 10110

Printed in the United States of America

10 9 8 7 6 5 4 3 2 1

ACKNOWLEDGMENTS

Many thanks to the following folks for sharing their local knowledge and patiently answering my questions: Jon Jarosh in Door County; Noreen Rueckert in Green County; Sharon Kaminecki at Earth Rider Cycling; Joy Rasin in Lake Geneva; Sue Anne Zollinger, pie maven; Ted Villaire, author of *60 Hikes within 60 Miles: Chicago* and the forthcoming *Road Biking Illinois*, *Camping Illinois*, and *Best Bike Rides Near Chicago*; Jennifer Denniston; Sam Benson; Brian Austin and Tim McKeon; Marie Erdman Bradshaw; Nancy Castagnet; Rose Spinelli; Frances Ginther; and Ray Zielinski.

Many, many thanks to Kim Grant for suggesting this book be written, and for help and encouraging nudges throughout the process.

Utter gratitude to Lisa Beran for womaning the wheel and being such a swell road trip pal. I'm sorry I made you eat all that pie and ice cream.

And of course, this book would never have come to be without Eric Markowitz, my partner-for-life, who not only fed me, drove me, and edited my words, but also went on 20-mile bike rides, picked blue berries, slept in log cabins, and engaged in many other activities he did not bargain for. He's the ultimate traveling companion and deserves much more than just his backside in all my photos.

GREAT ESCAPES
Chicago

N

0 MILES 50

10 Door County

Green Bay

Wausau

Oshkosh

Fond du Lac

Cadillac

Ludington

Grand Rapids

Lake Michigan

6 Wisconsin Dells

5 Madison

2 Milwaukee

Racine

Saugatuck **7**

Kalamazoo

Monroe **1**

Dubuque

20 Lake Geneva

Rockford

Waukegan

16. Chicago Botanic Garden
3. Devon Avenue
11. Oak Park
4. Pilsen

17 Galena

19 Rock River Valley

Aurora

16 **3**
11
4
Chicago

Gary

8 Harbor Country

MICH.

Davenport

15 Quad Cities

18 Starved Rock

9

IND.

South Bend

12 Amish Country

Galesburg

13 Pontiac

Indiana Dunes

Fort Wayne

Peoria

Bloomington

Lafayette

Muncie

Champaign

14 Springfield

Decatur

Indianapolis

WISC.
ILL.

ILL.
IND.

MICH.
WISC.

Paul Woodward, © The Countryman Press

CONTENTS

INTRODUCTION

Chicago is, of course, one of the world's great cities, and millions of visitors flock here each year to get a piece of our action. So it must seem odd that we're writing a book about how to *leave* this fine metropolis.

But sometimes the urge strikes to spend the night in a town with 500 people instead of 3 million. Or in a place where you can see the stars and smell the pines. Or in a spot where you can surf a phat wave, or eat a fat slice of pie.

This book helps you find those places. We've divided the destinations into four themes. "Eat" sites revolve around food and/or drink, where you can buy cheese and beer at the source or immerse yourself in an ethnic cuisine. "Play" covers good-time, beachy trips where you can also hike, bike, and paddle. "Learn" getaways have a historic or cultural component. "Chill" escapes are nature-filled places to relax. The themes are not binding, though, so don't get too stuck on the label. You'll find plenty of good chow in "Learn" destinations, and biking and kayaking jaunts in "Eat" locales. "Fast Breaks" are destinations within a half hour of downtown—including two that are in the city, but feel much farther away.

You're probably familiar with most of the destinations listed. Our goal is not to surprise you with new places, but to put a fresh light on the standbys. Maybe you'll visit Galena in January to ski. Or Starved Rock in February to hike to ice falls. More than anything, we want to inspire you and give you the tools to hit the road. Haven't you always wanted to drive Route 66? Or see the Racing Sausages in Milwaukee? Or poke through Indiana's Amish Country?

Now's the time. Take a Great Escape.

EAT

1 • GREEN COUNTY'S CHEESE BOUNTY

Don't know your artisanal from farmstead, Gruyere from Gouda, curd from whey? A road trip to southern Wisconsin's Green County will sort you out. The area is home to the largest concentration of cheesemakers in the nation.

The reason they're all bunched here is simple: the land. Green County sits at the edge of the Driftless Region, which glaciers bypassed during the last ice age. Instead of getting flattened, the landscape was left with hills, valleys, and limestone-rich soil. Today the distinctive land grows distinctive grass, which makes distinctive food for cows, and that results in distinctive milk that creates distinctive cheese. Got it? Old World Europeans did, particularly the Swiss. They flocked to the region in the 1800s, bringing their cheesemaking skills with them.

So unloosen the belt. The average American eats 31 pounds of cheese each year, and you'll bite into a hefty portion of that amount as you tour through cow-splotched fields and visit the local masters at work.

Before embarking, let's get straight on some cheesy terminology. *Artisanal* refers to cheese made in small batches. *Farmstead* means cheese made with milk from the farmer's own herd. *Curds* are milk solids separated from the *whey* (a.k.a. liquid) when milk is coagulated. And fresh curds *squeak* when you bite into them. Sadly, they lose this attribute after about 12 hours—which is why it's vital to get curds hot off the press.

But you don't have to be a diehard cheesehead to appreciate Green County. Its back roads and car-free bike trails lure both novice and experienced cyclists. They're eager to roll by scenic barns, bovines, and hay bales sun-dappled enough to be a Monet painting. In summer, visitors tube and canoe down the Sugar River and watch movies at the local drive-in. In fall, they come to see the white ash, red oak, sugar maple, and hickory trees explode in color.

Monroe (population 10,800) is the biggest town and county seat, filled with cheese history and

Limburger taverns, but it's nicer to snooze in the smaller towns. Brodhead (population 3,100) makes a good base due to its funky cycling hotel and walkable town center with pizza, Chinese food, and Pabst Blue Ribbon bars. Swiss-themed New Glarus (population 2,100) adds cowbells, cuckoo clocks, and a lip-smacking microbrewery to the mix.

■ ■ ■ ■ GETTING THERE

Monroe is 135 miles northwest of Chicago. Take I-90 west out of the city (tolls apply). Just before Rockford follow I-39 and US 51 heading south for 3 miles, and then merge onto US 20 heading west. Stay on the highway for about 30 miles to Freeport, and then turn onto IL 26 heading north. At the Wisconsin border, the road becomes WI 69, and it runs into Monroe. The trip takes two and a half to three hours.

■ ■ ■ ■ GETTING AROUND

From Monroe, Brodhead lies 16 miles east via WI 11, while New Glarus lies 16 miles north via WI 69. Madison is 28 miles beyond New Glarus to the north.

If you're biking, remember the farther west you go in the area, the hillier it gets.

■ ■ ■ ■ WHERE TO STAY

Earth Rider Hotel (608-897-8300, 866-245-5276; www.earth ridercycling.com), 929 West Exchange Street, Brodhead. Attached to the bike shop below, this bold-colored, five-room property wows with pillow-top mattresses, goat-milk soaps, flat-screen TVs, DVD players, wireless access, and mod furnishings made out of recycled bike gear. It's the ultimate soft landing after a hard day of cycling on the nearby Sugar River Trail. The property uses natural cleaners and low-VOC paints. Rooms including continental breakfast cost $70—130.

Inn Serendipity (608-329-7056; www.innserendipity.com), 7843 County Road P, Browntown (8 miles west of Monroe). This two-room B&B is part of a 5-acre working organic farm. The owners are serious about sustainable liv-

Biking through a covered bridge on the Sugar River Trail near Brodhead

ing and power the house using solar and wind systems. They use natural-fiber sheets and towels and all-natural cleaning products. Rooms including vegetarian breakfast cost $105–120.

Chalet Landhaus (608-527-5234, 800-944-1716; www.chalet landhaus.com), 801 WI 69, New Glarus. The rooms are dated, but the hotel's straight-from-the-Alps ambience tries hard to make up for it. Rooms come in several configurations, including those with a Jacuzzi, private balcony, or multiple beds for large families. There's an indoor pool, sauna, and wireless Internet (though access can be sketchy). It's located right by the Sugar River trailhead. Rooms including breakfast cost $99–155, suites $155–180.

▪▪▪▪ CAMPING

New Glarus Woods State Park (608-527-2335; www.dnr.state.wi .us/org/land/parks), W5446 County Road NN (2 miles south of town via WI 69). Open year-round. Voted Wisconsin's best park to view a moonrise, small New Glarus Woods has 32 primitive campsites (18 drive-in and 14 walk-in). There are no showers, just water hydrants and pit toilets. Cyclists often camp here, as the park connects to the Sugar River Trail via a mile-long dedicated path. Park entry by car requires a vehicle permit, which costs $10/day or $35/year; cyclists get in for free. Reservations (888-947-2757; www.reserveamerica .com) are accepted for a $10 fee. Campsites cost $14.

▪▪▪▪ EATING OUT

Baumgartner's Cheese Store and Tavern (608-325-6157), 1023 Sixteenth Avenue, Monroe. Open daily 8 AM–11 PM. This old Swiss tavern on the town square provides an experience you won't find anywhere else: biting into a fresh Limburger-and-raw-onion sandwich. Zowie! Less adventuresome eaters can opt for several other types of cheese sandwiches, accompanied by a swell local brew selection. Don't forget to ask the friendly staff about the dollar on the ceiling trick. Sandwiches, $4–7.

New Glarus Bakery (608-527-2916), 534 First Street, New Glarus. Open daily 7 AM–5 PM. The bakery's artisan breads go mighty well with all that cheese you've just bought. Breads, $3–4.

Tastee Crème (608-897-8745), 208 1st Center Avenue, Brodhead. Open daily 12 PM–9 PM. Follow the line of cars to this forlorn little white trailer, and you'll find 50-cent cones swirled high with soft-serve ice cream.

Country Lane Bakery (608-897-3820), 1602 Scotch Hill Road,

Brodhead. Open Fri. and Sat. 8 AM—6 PM. Specialties at this Amish bakery include lemon cream pie and cheddar-swirled bread. Breads, $3—4.

■■■■ WHAT TO SEE AND DO

DIY cheese tours: Visiting local cheesemakers lets you get the goods fresh from the source and for supercheap prices. Most places sell their wares from big refrigerators out front. However, getting an actual tour of cheese-makers' facilities is difficult, given liability issues and limited staff time. If you call ahead, you'll stand a better chance. The *Dairyland* map (see Resources, page 18) can guide you. Mornings Monday through Thursday are typically the best times, though be understanding if a cheesemaker can't grant your request. They're busy people!

A good place to start is **Decatur Dairy** (608-897-8661; www.decaturdairy.com), W1668 County Road F, Brodhead. Open Mon. through Sat. 9 AM—5 PM, tours weekdays 9 AM—11 AM. These folks make 28,000 pounds of cheese per day, with Havarti and curds among their specialties. What's most amazing is they'll give you an impromptu, full-on tour—one of the only cheesemak-ers to do so.

You can watch cheesemakers in action weekday mornings from the observation deck at **Roth Kase** (608-328-2122; www.rothkase .com), 657 Second Street, Monroe. Open Mon. through Fri. 9 AM—6 PM, Sat. 9 AM—5 PM, Sun. 10 AM—5 PM. It's not the same as being on the floor at Decatur Dairy, but it'll do. Roth Kase wins serious points for its Buttermilk Blue. Plunge into the "overstock" cooler for blocks of it for as little as $1.

Rolling out the barrels at New Glarus Brewery
PHOTOGRAPH BY LISA BERAN

After a hard day of backroad biking, you've earned your Tastee Crème.

Other area cheesemakers who sometimes do tours if you reserve ahead are **Franklin Cheese** (608-325-3725), W7256 Franklin Road, Monroe; and **Silver-Lewis** (608-938-4813), W3075 County Road EE, Monticello. Another place worth your time is **Chalet Cheese Co-op** (608-325-4343), N4858 County Road N, Monroe—it's the nation's only Limburger plant.

Organized cheese tours: **Learn Great Foods** (866-240-1650; www .learngreatfoods.com), based near Galena, Illinois, visits southern Wisconsin cheesemakers. See chapter 17 for details.

Brewery tours: It's a crime not to stop and sample the suds at **New Glarus Brewery** (608-527-5850; www.newglarusbrewing .com), County Road W, New Glarus. Open daily 10 AM—5 PM. Wander through on a self-guided tour, chat with the brewmaster, and learn the secret ingredient in the flagship Spotted Cow ale. Tours cost $3.50 per person, including three samples and a commemorative glass.

Biking: The first thing to do to get the wheels moving is ring up **Bike Green County** (888-222-9111; www.greencounty.org/bike_ride .iml). Tell them when and where you'd like to ride, and they'll plan the whole shebang. They'll customize a backroad and/or trail route (looping from 20 to 80

miles, so you'll start and end in the same place), supply street-by-street directions and maps, arrange lodging and luggage transfer, and provide emergency roadside assistance, starting at $80 per person per day. The group does a great job, and letting them plan your trek—and schlep your bags—is highly recommended. If you need to rent bikes, add $15 per day (and note you'll have to start your journey in Brodhead versus elsewhere in the county).

Another tremendous resource is **Earth Rider Cycling Boutique** (608-897-8300, 866-245-5276; www.earthridercycling.com), 929 West Exchange Street, Brodhead. It's a full-service bike shop and small hotel, and owner Sharon Kaminecki is a fountain of knowledge who can help you plot routes around Brodhead to Amish businesses, emu farms, and even cheese shops, as well as answer trail questions. This is also the place to pick up local trail maps and buy trail passes. Bike rentals cost $15 per day.

Two main trails crisscross the county. The **Sugar River Trail** spans 23 flat miles from Brodhead to New Glarus. It follows an old railroad line over trestle bridges and through farmland, woods, and meadows. The **Badger Trail** offers more dramatic scenery

▮▮▮▮ BEER AND CHEESE: TOGETHER AT LAST

Sure, there's wine and cheese. But you're in beer territory, so let's revise the tradition.

Ales and lagers blend artfully with most cheese types, so you can't go too far wrong when pairing. Just remember to bring the cheese to room temperature to open up the flavors, and don't serve the beers ice cold.

Here are the matchups: Pair aged cheddar with stouts; goat cheese with wheat beers; bleu cheese with Lambic or fruit beers; and Colby, fontina, Gouda, and other semisoft cheese with brown ales.

including an amazing tunnel (bring a flashlight), limestone bluffs, and rolling countryside on its level, 33-mile route from the Illinois border to 7 miles south of Madison (the final miles into the city are scheduled for completion sometime in 2009). The two trails meet near the town of Monticello. The **Cheese Country Trail** also runs through the area, but it's shared with ATVs and not nearly as bike friendly. Trail passes cost $4 per day, $20 per year; buy them at local businesses or leave your money in the trailhead drop-box.

Movie watching: **Sky Vu Drive-In Theater** (608-325-4200; www.goetzskyvu.com), N1936 WI 69, on Monroe's southern outskirts, screens first-run flicks under the stars. Bring lawn chairs and a portable radio (to play the sound), and you'll greatly

enhance your viewing pleasure. Tickets cost $7 for adults, $4.50 for children.

Tubing and canoeing: For a lazy trip down the Sugar River, plop your butt in an inner tube or paddle a canoe or kayak from **S&B** (608-862-3933; www.badger-trail.com/SB-tubing.htm), 100 East Main Street, Albany. Open daily 10 AM–8 PM. The ride downstream takes two to three hours, and you'll return via shuttle van. The cost is $12/15/20 per tube/kayak/canoe.

▮▮▮▮ HISTORIC SITES

Historic Cheesemaking Center (608-325-4636), 2108 Sixth Avenue, Monroe (by the corner of WI 69 and 21st Street). Open daily 9 AM–4 PM Mar. through mid-Nov. Learn how cheese is made on a guided tour through old milking machines, churns, and copper kettles. Honey Belle the cow statue provides sweet photo opportunities. The building also serves as the Green County Welcome Center, where you can pick up area maps, brochures, and bike trail passes. Suggested donation is $2.

▪▪▪▪ DON'T FORGET

Bring a hefty cooler to keep cheese purchases fresh during your drive home.

▪▪▪▪ SPECIAL EVENTS

Late July: Amish Quilt Auction (www.greencounty.org), Brodhead.

Late September: Cheese Days (www.cheesedays.com), Monroe. The town fetes its favorite foodstuff in even-numbered years.

Late September: Oktoberfest (www.swisstown.com), New Glarus. Chainsaw carving, sausage making, and local brew drinking merge into a rollicking celebration.

▪▪▪▪ NEARBY

Angelic Organics (815-389-8455; www.learngrowconnect.org), 1547 Rockton Road, Caledonia, Illinois (32 miles southeast of Brodhead). Adults and kids alike learn to compost, keep bees, make goat-milk soap, and build solar water heaters at this organic farm. The owner has an intriguing backstory—see the PBS documentary *The Real Dirt on Farmer John*, available on DVD. Workshops typically cost $10 to $80.

Mt. Horeb is a Norwegian-influenced community 18 miles north of New Glarus. It's famous for its trolls, Mustard Museum (800-438-6878; www.mustard museum.com), and Tyrol Basin Ski Resort (608-437-4754; www.tyrolbasin.com).

Mineral Point is a Cornish-influenced community about 30 miles west of New Glarus. Its artists' galleries and Brewery Creek Inn B&B (608-987-3298; www.brewerycreek.com) draw visitors looking to sink back in time (and drink beer).

▪▪▪▪ RESOURCES

Green County Tourism (888-222-9111; www.greencounty.org). The Visitors Guide is packed with useful maps, bike routes, and other info.

Wisconsin Milk Marketing Board (608-836-8820; www.wis dairy.com). Contact the board to receive the free *Traveler's Guide to America's Dairyland*, a map of cheesemakers and sellers throughout the state.

Living on the Wedge DVD (www.livingonthewedge.com). Food writer Mariana Coyne visits southern Wisconsin's cheesemakers to get the inside scoop on how they craft their wares. It's a delicious way to see how cheese is made. It's not available in libraries, but you can order it online for $19.95 or sometimes catch it on local PBS channels.

Cheese Underground (http://cheeseunderground.blog spot.com). This blog by Madisonite Jeanne Carpenter gives the gossip on Wisconsin's specialty cheesemakers.

The Cheeses of Wisconsin: A Culinary Travel Guide by Jeanette Hurt (Countryman Press: 2008). Ms. Hurt knows her cheese. She interviews cheesemakers throughout the state, including several around Green County, about how they make their specialty products. The descriptions, photos, and recipes will make you want to lick the page.

2 • WHAT'S BREWING IN MILWAUKEE

It's no surprise Milwaukee ranks second among America's hardest drinking cities (this according to a 2008 *Forbes* study). After all, the town was built on beer, and there was a time in the late 19th century when 80 small breweries were boiling up suds.

Eventually, these beer-makers merged into the big three—Pabst, Miller, and Schlitz—and Milwaukee became the country's top beer-producing city, garnering nicknames like "Brew City" and "the nation's watering hole." The industry was even on TV each week, when Laverne and Shirley capped beer bottles on the much-loved 1970s show.

Beer still forms the backbone of a visit to town. Tours of the mega Miller plant and craft brewers like Lakefront and Sprecher are a must-do. Baseball fans will want to see the Brewers play baseball at Miller Park. And beer-filled bashes fill downtown's festival grounds most weekends, letting locals make merry and listen to live music.

If beer's not your thing, though, no worries: the Art Museum alone is worth the trip to Milwaukee, as is the new Harley Museum celebrating all things motorcycle.

What's more, somewhere along the way Milwaukee morphed from a workingman's town to a place where hipsters play, at least in certain neighborhoods. These areas guarantee a good meal, which is helpful after all the beer. Hot spots include downtown's North Old World 3rd Street, lined with old-school sausage shops and eateries; stylish Brady Street north of downtown, a road of indie coffee shops, secondhand stores, fashionable boutiques, and ethnic restaurants; the gentrified Third Ward at downtown's southern edge, a warehouse district made over with sidewalk cafés and art galleries; and Bay View, a southern neighborhood with swank bars and cafés strung out along Kinnickinnic Avenue.

Milwaukee strikes an unusual and admirable balance between high culture and earthy pleasures, and the result is just a plain ol' good time. Did you expect anything less from a town where 70.6 percent of residents (*Forbes* again) knocked back at least one drink in the last 30 days?

▪▪▪▪ GETTING THERE

Milwaukee is 92 miles north of Chicago. Take I-90/94 west from downtown, and follow I-94 west when it splits off. The interstate goes almost all the way into Milwaukee. It's a busy road, and travel times can be atrocious during peak hours. It's also a toll road, so get ready to pony up $2.50. Just south of Milwaukee I-94 merges with I-43, and you'll follow I-43 north for the final few miles toward downtown. Exit 72C for Kilbourn Avenue is a handy one for downtown's hotels. The trip takes one and a half to two hours.

Public transportation is also an option. **Amtrak** (800-872-7245; www.amtrak.com) runs the "Hiawatha" train seven times per day between Chicago and Milwaukee. The trip takes one and a half hours and costs $22 one way. Milwaukee's station is located downtown at 433 West St. Paul Avenue.

Megabus (877-462-6342; www.megabus.com/us) runs frequent express buses from Chicago to Milwaukee; drop-off is at the Amtrak station. The trip takes two hours and costs $11 one way.

▪▪▪▪ GETTING AROUND

Milwaukee's sights and neighborhoods are a bit far-flung. They're walkable if you're with hardy souls, but you'll likely end up driving to certain destinations and paying meters. For reference, the Milwaukee Art Museum on the lakefront downtown is about 1.5 miles from North Old World 3rd Street, 1.75 miles from Brady Street, 1 mile from the Third Ward, 4 miles from Bay View, and 5 miles from Miller Park.

The **Milwaukee County Transit System** (414-344-6711) provides local bus service. Rides cost $2; day passes are not available. Useful routes are Bus 90 to Miller Park and Bus 31 to Miller Brewery. Catch both of them along Wisconsin Avenue. A free trolley runs downtown in summer.

▪▪▪▪ WHERE TO STAY

Comfort Inn and Suites Downtown Lakeshore (414-276-8800, 800-328-7275; www.choicehotels

The Milwaukee Art Museum's distinctive "wing" moves, see it open and close daily at noon.

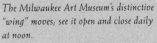

.com), 916 East State Street. The Comfort Inn is a terrific value in a terrific location near the lake, with comfy beds, contemporary furnishings, free in-room wireless access, and a free buffet each morning. When touring indie bands come to town, this is where they crash, so the hotel has earned hipster cachet—though you'll also find families staying here taking advantage of the good deal. Keep in mind it's still a Comfort Inn, but it's something for the genre. Rooms including breakfast cost $130–170; parking costs $10.

Hotel Metro (414-272-1937, 877-638-7620; www.hotelmetro .com), 411 East Mason Street. The restored-deco Metro is Milwaukees's top mod address, and it's right smack downtown. All rooms are wireless-equipped suites, with a curved wall that separates the bedroom and its soft linens from the sitting area and its high-def, flat-screen TV. The rooftop spa and chic café/lounge add to the Euro vibe. Guests also get free bicycles to use. Rooms cost $219–269, parking costs $25.

Brumder Mansion (414-342-9767, 866-793-3676; www .brumdermansion.com), 3046 West Wisconsin Avenue (about 3 miles west of downtown). This six-room B&B, in a big, old, slightly spooky Victorian manor

that's antiqued to the hilt, is a little off the tourist track, but not bad if you have a car. Though rough around the edges, the neighborhood is fine. Brumder offers a full breakfast downstairs, or it can provide a "breakfast basket" for private, in-room dining. Rooms including breakfast cost $130–200.

▪▪▪▪ EATING OUT

The Friday night fish fry is a tradition observed at restaurants all over Milwaukee and throughout Wisconsin. If you're in town at the workweek's end, check out one like the rip-roaring fry at Lakefront Brewery (see What to See and Do, page 24). It's a great place to mingle with locals.

Trocadero (414-272-0205), 1758 North Water Street. Open Mon. through Fri. 11 AM–12 AM, Sat. and Sun. 9 AM–12 AM. This romantic, French-influenced coffeehouse/ restaurant/bar oozes style—not surprising since it's right by Brady Street. The year-round patio (it's heated in winter) jumps with patrons showing their joie de vivre while eating crepes, baguettes with jam, mussels and frites, and cheese plates, accompanied by stellar wines. Mains, $7–17.

Roots Restaurant and Cellar (414-374-8480), 1818 North Hubbard Street (across the river from

Brady Street). The restaurant is open for lunch Mon. through Fri. II AM—2 PM; for dinner Mon. through Thurs. 5 PM—9 PM, Fri. and Sat. 5 PM—10 PM; and for brunch Sun. 10 AM—2 PM. The Cellar is open for dinner only (same hours as the restaurant), though the bar serves drinks until 2 AM. The chefs are Slow Food proponents who grow many of Roots' vegetables on their nearby farm. The sleek main dining room upstairs serves pricier fare, like soy-grilled tilapia with cashew sticky rice. Downstairs in the nifty Cellar—a candlelit room where sculpted metal vines cover the ceiling— unusual small plates like the butterbean-peanut corn dog and jerk pulled-pork sandwich go down the hatch. The patio's Adirondack chairs provide the ideal spot to river-gaze while sipping from the lengthy beer, wine, and cocktail list. Small plates, $8—15; mains, $19—36.

Watts Tea Room (414-290-5720), 761 North Jefferson Street. Open Mon. through Sat. 9 AM—4 PM. Watts is a great, quirky breakfast and lunch eatery downtown, above a china shop. It's very "ladies luncheon," and famous for its ginger toast. To get the full experience, come for afternoon tea, when the requisite finger sandwiches, pastries, and scones hit the tables between 2 PM and 3:45 PM every day except Sun. Breakfast, $7—8; lunch mains, $10—15; afternoon tea, $16.

Leon's (414-383-1784), 3131 South 27th Street (5 miles southwest of downtown). Open daily II AM—12 AM. Don't dare leave town without trying the Milwaukee specialty, frozen custard. It's like ice cream, only smoother and richer thanks to extra egg yolks being whipped in. Leon's has scooped the goods since 1942, and looks the part with its old-time drive-in building bathed in neon. Many custard aficionados say Leon's makes the best, but others say the honor goes to **Kopp's** (414-961-2006), 5373 North Port Washington Road (in suburban Glendale, about 7 miles north of downtown). It's open daily 10:30 AM—11:30 PM. Kopp's schtick is to advertise flavors of the day (Midnight Chocolate Cake! Grand Marnier Blueberry Crisp!) from a flashing highway billboard and lure drivers into its futuristic, steely dwelling. The jury is split, so you'll have to try both custards and decide for yourself. A scoop at either place costs around $2.

▓▓▓▓ DRINKING

Lakefront Brewery (see What to See and Do, below). This is an option on Friday nights only, but it's a beauty.

Palm Tavern (414-744-0393), 2989 South Kinnickinnic Avenue (4 miles south of downtown). Open Mon. through Sat. from 5 PM, Sun. from 7 PM. Located in the south side neighborhood of Bay View, the dark, funky Palm carries a huge selection of unusual beers (with a focus on Belgian brews) and single-malt scotches. If the guy behind the counter looks familiar, it's because he's Bruno Johnson, former barman at the Hopleaf and Green Mill in Chicago.

Kochanski's Concertina Beer Hall (414-837-6552), 1920 South 37th Street (5 miles southwest of downtown). Open Tues. through Fri. from 4 PM, Sat. from 12 PM. Hipsters and old-timers alike twirl around the floor to live polka music at kitschy Kochanski's. The big beer selection rocks, too, with everything from Wisconsin microbrews to Schlitz to Polish standbys on tap or in bottles. There are free dance lessons on Thurs. at 7 PM, and usually no cover charge on the other nights.

Von Trier (414-272-1775), 2235 North Farwell Avenue (2 miles north of downtown). Open daily from 4 PM. Von Trier is a Milwaukee classic, a rustic German beer hall with a mighty European brew list and a fun beer garden in back.

Only in Milwaukee will you find such a cheesy motorcycle.

Riverfront seating at Lakefront Brewery during the Friday night fish fry

▪▪▪▪ WHAT TO SEE AND DO

Brewery tours: Schlitz ("the beer that made Milwaukee famous"), Pabst, and Miller were all based here at one time, but among the majors, only Miller—or Miller-Coors, as it's now called—remains. Several small breweries have emerged to pick up the slack. The best tours include:

Miller Brewing Company (414-

931-2337; www.millercoors.com), 4251 West State Street. Tours held Mon. through Sat. 10:30 AM–3:30 PM, but the schedule can change, so it's best to call ahead. You might not think much of Miller's suds, but the mondo facility is something to behold. You'll see the packaging plant, where 2,000 cans are filled each minute, and the warehouse, where a half-million cases chill while awaiting shipment. The tasting session at the tour's end provides a generous ration of three full-size samples. Don't forget your ID. The 60-minute tours are free.

Lakefront Brewery (414-372-8800; www.lakefrontbrewery .com), 1872 North Commerce Street (across the river from Brady Street). Tours held Mon. through Fri. at 2 PM and 3 PM; Sat. at 1 PM, 2 PM, and 3 PM; and Sun. (during summer only) at 2 PM. You have to pay for Lakefront's tours, but they include a commemorative pint glass, four tasty 6-ounce samples, and a coupon for a free brewski at a local bar. Friday night is a prime time to visit, since the brewery hosts a festive fish fry in its cavernous banquet hall from 4 PM to 9 PM. The place fills to the rafters with seniors, kids, and stylish 20-somethings eating beer-battered cod ($9.95) and swinging to the live polka band. It's fine to come for a drink

only; the hall has 16 of its beers on tap, of which the Organic ESB wins special praise. If the polka tunes get to be too much, take your beer out back (walk past the EXIT sign behind the band) and sip at Lakefront's outdoor tables by the river. Loads of boaters tie up here and join the party. The brewery holds additional tours between 6 PM and 8 PM during the Friday fry, plus an environmental tour at 3:30 PM. The 60-minute tours cost $6.

Sprecher Brewing Company (414-964-2739; www.sprecher brewery.com), 701 West Glendale Avenue (6 miles north of downtown). Tours held Mon. through Fri. at 4pm, Sat. and Sun. at 12 PM, 1 PM, and 2 PM. The small microbrewery's tour includes a museum of memorabilia from long-gone Milwaukee suds-makers and a beer garden with oompah music. Because the company also produces root beer and sodas, kids are welcome. The tour includes four beer samples (Hefe Weiss and Black Bavarian are usually on tap), unlimited soda samples (orange, cream, cherry, etc.), and a commemorative glass. You must reserve in advance. Tours cost $4 for adults, $2 for kids.

Milwaukee Art Museum (414-224-3200; www.mam.org), 700 North Art Museum Drive. Open daily 10 AM–5 PM, Thurs. to 8 PM.

Even those who don't like art museums are wowed by this lakeside stunner. The winglike design by Santiago Calatrava has become a Milwaukee landmark. It soars open and closed every day at noon; the best place to see it in action is outside on the entrance ramp, about halfway down. Visitors are also allowed to walk in and see Windover Hall (a.k.a. the "wing") for free. If you decide to pay the admission fee and see the collection—which you should—it includes a permanent display on Frank Lloyd Wright and fantastic folk- and outsider-art galleries. Themed brochures at the front desk direct you to the museum's "Naughty Bits" (i.e., nudie artworks) and works to "Impress the Out-of-Towners" (highlights of the collection). Admission costs $8 for adults, $4 for children.

Harley-Davidson Museum (877-436-8738; www.h-dmuseum .com), 400 West Canal Street. Open daily 9 AM—6 PM, Wed. to 8 PM May through Oct., open Mon. through Fri. 10 AM—5 PM, Sat. and Sun. 9 AM—6 PM Nov. through Apr. In 1903 William Harley and Arthur Davidson, local Milwaukee schoolmates, built and sold their first Harley-Davidson motorcycle. This brand spankin' new museum, opened in July 2008, pays homage to the ballyhooed bikes. The industrial, glass-and-steel building sprawls across 20 riverfront acres just south of downtown and contains the Harley archives and a bike restoration facility in addition to a whole lotta motorcycles. Hog-heads go wild flashing pix of Harley's very first bike—the rattletrap Serial #1—as well as hundreds of other bikes that show styles through the ages. Even non-Harley owners will find much to love, because who doesn't long to see the bikes of Elvis and Evel Knievel? If you arrive by hog, you get special parking right by the entrance. Cars must park across the street in the lot. Kids get stoked by the free scavenger hunt activity bag; ask for it at the audio tour desk. Admission costs $16 for adults, $10 for children.

Can't get enough of the big, bad bikes? Take a tour of the **Harley-Davidson Plant** (414-343-7850; www.harley-davidson.com), 11700 West Capitol Drive (in the suburb of Wauwatosa, about 20 minutes northwest of downtown). Tours are offered Mon. through Fri. 9 AM—2 PM, but call ahead as sometimes the production schedule changes and tours are canceled. This plant—one of four in the nation—is where the engines are built. The one-hour excursion is more technical than whimsical, but at the end you get to sit in the saddle of a vintage bike. No

■ ■ ■ ■ **KNOW YOUR RACING SAUSAGES**

The five meats vying for supremacy during the sixth-inning footrace at Miller Park are Frank, the all-American hot dog sporting a baseball uniform; Bret the Bratwurst in green lederhosen; Stosh, the Polish dog in sunglasses; Guido, an Italian sausage donning a chef's hat; and Cinco the Chorizo, wearing a sombrero. Statistically speaking, Frank the hot dog wins the most races each year. Poor Cinco wins the fewest.

open-toed shoes are permitted. Tours are free.

Miller Park (414-902-4000; www.milwaukeebrewers.com), 1 Brewers Way, near South 46th Street (about 5 miles west of downtown). The Milwaukee Brewers play at this shiny ballpark that has a retractable roof and real grass. It's famous for its "Racing Sausages," a group of people in giant foam-rubber meat costumes who sprint down the field in the middle of the sixth inning. As if that's not reason enough to go, the concession stands sell hot dogs and bratwursts slathered with Secret Stadium Sauce (a barbeque-meets-sauerkraut-juice concoction that tastes much better than it sounds). Arrive early to partake of the raucous tailgating scene. Tickets cost $14–45.

Milwaukee Public Market (414-336-1111; www.milwaukee publicmarket.org), 400 North Water Street. Open Mon. through Fri. 10 AM–8 PM, Sat. and Sun. 8 AM–6 PM. Fresh and prepared foods fill the stalls at this year-round, indoor market in the Third Ward. Browse among cheeses, chocolates, spices, roasted coffees, and wines, or pick up soup, sushi, or sandwiches for a take-out lunch. The market also hosts events such as wine tastings, cooking classes, and live music. On Saturdays from mid-June through late October, an outdoor market sets up in the adjacent lot and adds seasonal produce and artworks to the mix. Admission is free.

Eisner Museum of Advertising and Design (414-847-3290; www .eisnermuseum.org), 208 North Water Street. Open Wed. 11 AM–5 PM, Thurs. 11 AM–8 PM, Fri. 11 AM–5 PM, Sat. 12 PM–5 PM, Sun. 1 PM–5 PM. Visitors often overlook this thought-provoking little museum with rotating exhibits on how advertising and design influence today's culture. You might see displays on the Frisch's Big Boy, Guinness ads through the ages, controversial presidential commercials, or PETA's "I'd Rather Go Naked Than Wear Fur" campaign. It's located in the Third Ward. Admission costs $5 for adults, $3 for children.

Fonzie Statue, on the Riverwalk (east side of the Milwaukee River, just south of Wells Street). Aayy, it's a life-size bronze Arthur Fonzarelli (a.k.a. The Fonz) from TV's *Happy Days*. The show, which ran from 1974 to 1984, was set in Milwaukee, and the city decided to honor the cool character with a statue. It's fast becoming Milwaukee's premier photo op.

▪▪▪▪ SPECIAL EVENTS

Milwaukee hosts rawkin' festivals practically every weekend. Most take place downtown at the lakefront Henry W. Maier Festival Park.

Late June: Summerfest (www .summerfest.com). The granddaddy of Milwaukee's fests, with more than 700 bands on a dozen stages over the course of 11 days in late June and early July. Very big names in country, blues, rock, and soul headline nightly.

Late June: Polish Fest (www .polishfest.org). Three days of pierogi cooking demonstrations, vodka tastings, a Chopin piano competition, and an open-air mass.

Late July: German Fest (www .germanfest.com). Four days of strudel, schnitzel, and steins of beer.

Mid-August: Irish Fest (www .irishfest.com). Four days of pennywhistles, step dancing, and Jameson whiskey.

▪▪▪▪ NEARBY

Cedarburg (www.cedarburg.org) is an 1840s mill town about 20 miles north of Milwaukee. The original limestone and cream-colored brick buildings have been preserved downtown along Washington Avenue and now house restaurants, antique shops, specialty stores (including a winery), and historic inns. Take I-43 north to Exit 89 County Road C/West Pioneer Road. Drive west to Washington Avenue.

▪▪▪▪ RESOURCES

Milwaukee Visitors Center (800-554-1448; www.visitmilwaukee .org), 500 North Harbor Drive (in the Discovery World building). Open daily 9 AM–5 PM. It produces a Visitors Guide and several specialty guides (i.e., bikers' guide, shopping guide, brewery guide, etc.). The selection is better online than on-site at the visitors desk.

On Milwaukee (www.on milwaukee.com). Online source for traffic and weather updates, plus restaurant and entertainment reviews.

Shepherd Express (www .expressmilwaukee.com). Free weekly paper covering news, events, and culture. The Web site has good dining and concert reviews.

3 • FAST BREAK:
Devon Avenue Smorgasbord

Few streets in the world offer the chance to eat samosas, kosher pizza, and Georgian fruit pies in one progressive meal. Or buy a Bollywood soundtrack, a dreidel, and a picture of Mecca in a single shopping spree. But that's Devon Avenue on Chicago's far north side.

The 1.5-mile stretch between Ridge Road and Kedzie Avenue is known as the "International Marketplace." Starting from the east and moving west, it morphs from Pakistani to Indian to Russian to Orthodox Jewish. It's an amazing cultural hodgepodge—and even more remarkable considering residents live side by side in U.N.-worthy peace.

The road got its name from English settlers in the late 1800s, who dubbed it Devon after their native county of Devonshire. There's not much English about the place now, since changing waves of immigrants descended and left their mark.

The street's global eats are its most striking feature. Spicy, sweet, or savory; snacks, buffets, or meals; vegetarian or meaty—

it's all here, with exotic shops filling the space in between. Note that many businesses close on Tuesday.

Once you've stuffed your face and shopping bag, head to nearby Warren Park. You can shoot nine holes of golf and slug baseballs in summer, or ice skate and sled-ride in winter.

▪▪▪▪ GETTING THERE

Devon Avenue is about 9 miles north of downtown Chicago. To get there by public transportation, take the Brown Line train to Western and transfer to bus 49B North Western. Or take the Red Line to Morse and transfer to bus 155 Devon.

Parking can be a hassle. Most side streets are permit parking only; Maplewood Avenue (2532 west) is an exception worth trying. St. Timothy Church (6326 North Washtenaw Avenue) offers its parking lot for free Mon. through Fri. 5 PM—10 PM and weekends 12 PM—10 PM. Devon Avenue itself is usually chaos, with meters that must be fed seven days a week.

▌▌▌▌ EATING OUT

The eateries below span the globe as well as the street. They're listed in order from east to west, so you can start at Ghareeb Nawaz and graze your way through to Hashalom, sampling Pakistani, Indian, Georgian, Israeli, and Moroccan foods en route. Of course, you'll never be able to stomach this much at one time, so prepare for multiple visits to Devon Avenue. And don't feel limited to the restaurants listed below. There are many more worthy places—simply more than this book has room for.

Ghareeb Nawaz (773-761-5300), 2032 West Devon Avenue. Open daily 8 AM—2 AM. Let's be clear about one thing: this is a dive, a vinyl-floor, cracked-plastic-booth dive. But you won't find anywhere else that serves such massive portions at such ridiculously low prices. It's all part of keeping true to its name, which means "sustainer of the poor." Step up to the counter to order; they've posted pictures of the various dishes on the wall behind, which helps you know your *paratha* (flaky, hubcap-size, wheat tortilla-like wraps stuffed with scrambled eggs, vegetables, or charred meat) from your *biryani* (turmeric-seasoned rice dishes cooked with meat or veggies). The *thalis* (big plates with a little dip of several different dishes) are bigger than the children eating them. Mains, $2—4.50.

Lahore Food and Grill (773-761-4919), 2116 West Devon Avenue. Open daily 5 PM—6 AM. Pull up a chair with the cab-drivers at this no-frills Pakistani joint known for its KFC (Karachi Fried Chicken). The bird's proper

Fresh Farms market stacked high with fresh produce

name is *charga*, and it's a juicy and super-spiced finger-lickin' deal. Mains, $6–9.

Tiffin (773-338-2143), 2536 West Devon Avenue. Open daily 11:30 AM–3 PM and 5 PM–10 PM. Tiffin wins raves for its lunch buffet, an all-you-can-eat, white-tablecloth extravaganza that'll stuff meat eaters and vegetarians alike. The Indian spread typically has about 10 entrées, as well as a few appetizers and desserts. *Pakoras* (deep-fried, chickpea-battered veggies) and samosas (pyramid-shaped fried dough pockets stuffed with potatoes and peas) are good bets for the appetizers. Mains might be *daal makhani* (a seasoned lentil stew), *saag paneer* (cooked spinach with ricotta-like cheese cubes), *baigan* (eggplant), chicken or lamb curry, and tandoori chicken (cooked and seasoned in a special clay oven). Rice cushions the dishes, and you can sauce them with chutney (red is sweet; green is somewhat spicy) or *raita* (cool yogurt mixed with diced cucumbers and onions). Sweet picks for dessert include *gajar halwa* (shredded sweetened carrot), *kheer* (rice pudding), and *gulab jaman* (doughnut holes bobbing in thick syrup). This is also one of the few places on the street that serves alcohol. Buffet, $9.95 on weekdays, $10.95 on weekends.

Udupi Palace (773-338-2152), 2543 West Devon Avenue. Open daily 11:30 AM–10 PM. Owned by the same folks as Tiffin (see above), Udupi is the vegetarian sibling. There's no buffet here, but you'll walk away equally overfed from the giant, famed *masala dosai* (a kite-size rice-and-lentil crepe folded over a plopping of cumin-spiced potatoes and onion). Forgo the fork, and eat it by hand. Vegetable curries and rice dishes round out the menu. Mains, $7–10.

Sukhadia's (773-338-5400), 2559 West Devon Avenue. Open 9:30 AM–9:30 PM, closed Tues. Buttery sweets and savory snacks can be munched in equal measure at this bustling, counter-service eatery. Indian confections fill display cases in all their neon pink, green, orange, and yellow glory, colored by ingredients like pistachio, carrot, saffron, and coconut. Popular treats to try include *burfee* (sometimes spelled *barfi*), a mild fudge, and *jalebi*, pretzel-shaped fried wheat flour doused in syrup. For snacks, order the *bhel puri*, Bombay's famous street eat. It mixes puffed rice, onions, cilantro, potatoes, sev (tiny dried noodles), yogurt, and green-chili chutney into a sweet-and-sour mouth explosion. It's best to eat it right away, since crispness is key. Items, $4.99–7.99 per pound.

Fresh Farms Market (773-764-3557), 2626 West Devon Avenue. Open daily 7 AM—9:30 PM. A huge array of low-cost produce, sacks of dried beans, and packages of prepared Indian foods (including frozen dinners) make this the one-stop shop for do-it-yourself meals.

Kamdar Plaza (773-338-8100), 2646 West Devon Avenue. Open 11 AM—8 PM, closed Tues. In addition to all the groovy incense, this grocery store lines its shelves with dried lentils, canned chutneys, and other Indian goods. The snack counter cooks up specialties from India's northern state of Gujarat, such as *dhokla* (a savory spongy steamed cake of chickpea flour and yogurt) and *khandvi* (similar ingredients, but rolled like a tiny crepe and topped with cilantro, coconut, and mustard seeds). Items, $4.99—7.99 per pound.

Tel Aviv Kosher Pizza (773-764-3776), 6349 North California Avenue. Open Sun. through Thurs. 11 AM—11 PM, Fri. 11 AM—3 PM. "We serve all kinds of food for all kinds of Jews," the no-nonsense lady behind the counter says, as she takes your order. She's not kidding. Choose from Mexican dishes (enchiladas, $7.75), Chinese dishes (egg foo young, $4.50), Middle Eastern dishes (falafel plate, $5.95), and Italian dishes (spaghetti, $5.50; pizza, $1.93—2.70 per slice). The food is so-so, but the atmosphere is the real treat: Hassidic scholars eating a slice, groups of old men discussing politics, Orthodox women feeding their broods, and almost everyone speaking Hebrew. All dishes are kosher, of course, and fish is the only meat on the menu.

No fork required when eating masala dosai.

Need a sari? Devon Avenue's shops have you covered.

Argo Georgian Bakery (773-764-6322), 2812 West Devon Avenue. Open Mon. through Sat. 9 AM—7 PM, Sun. 9 AM—6 PM. An igloo-shaped clay oven dominates the room, producing spongy round flatbread ($2.50), *hachapuri* (puffed pastry filled with cheese, $2.70), single-serving fruit pies like cherry and blueberry ($1.70), and other sweet and savory treats from the old country. Items are to-go, though there are two small tables to sit at if you can't wait to tear in (which often happens with the hachapuri —it's that mouthwatering).

Hashalom (773-465-5675), 2905 West Devon Avenue. Open Wed. through Sun. 12 PM—9 PM. Hashalom breaks boundaries by serving Israeli-Moroccan cuisine in an American-diner atmosphere. Combo plates provide a sampler of the vegetarian dishes (i.e., Jerusalem salad, hummus, baba ganouj, eggplant, and perfectly crisped falafel for the Israeli plate; cooked tomatoes, eggplant, beets, carrot salad, and atomically spiced peppers for the Moroccan version). Meat eaters can carve into lamb kebabs, stuffed Cornish hen, or beef goulash. Couscous (veggie-style or with chicken) mixed with sweet almonds and raisins draws fans on Fri. and Sat. evenings. Mains, $6—10.

▪▪▪▪ SHOPPING

Devon Avenue holds almost as many stores as it does restaurants. Bollywood music, incense, cell phones and cards, electronics, colorful fabrics, and jangle-y bangles top the purchase list.

Indian sari and jewelry shops cluster near 2500 West Devon Avenue. A few blocks east they give way to a gaggle of electronics and dollar stores. To the west, Islamic goods shops—and beyond that, Jewish shops—line the street.

Kamdar Plaza (see Eating Out, above) is the place to go for incense. The selection includes sticks and cones to help you spice up your love life, make more money, or just freshen the abode.

Rosenblum's World of Judaica (773-262-1700), 2906 West Devon Avenue offers rows of dreidels, menorahs, yarmulkes, shofars, and other tchotchkes. It's open Mon. through Wed. 9 AM—6 PM, Thurs. 9 AM—7 PM, Fri. 9 AM—2 PM, and Sun 10 AM—4 PM.

▪▪▪▪ SPECIAL EVENTS

Diwali, also known as the Festival of Light, is a five-day celebration observed throughout the globe's Indian communities. On Devon Avenue, colorful decorations and special foods mark the occasion.

Dates vary, but it usually takes place in October or November.

▮▮▮▮ NEARBY

Work off all those samosas at **Warren Park** (773-262-6314), 6601 North Western Avenue, a couple blocks north of the Devon. It's one of Chicago's best-endowed playlands, where you can golf, skate, sled, or slug baseballs.

To tee off at the nine-hole **Robert A. Black Golf Course** (reservations 312-245-0909 or www.cpdgolf.com), enter from pro shop at 2045 West Pratt Avenue. The course is open during daylight hours year-round, weather permitting. The cost is $16.25 on weekdays, $17.75 on weekends.

Practice your home-run swing at the **baseball batting cages**. They're open Tues. through Fri. 4 PM–7:30 PM, Sat. and Sun. 11 AM–3:30 PM Apr. through early Sept. It's best to bring your own bat and helmet, though a limited supply is sometimes available from the person who's working on-site. Fifteen pitches cost $1; get tokens from the machine inside the field house (it accepts $1 and $5 bills only).

The **outdoor ice rink** (773-761-8663) is behind the field house. It offers open skate time Wed. through Fri. 3 PM–7:30 PM, Sat. and Sun. 12:30 PM–7:30 PM late November through mid-Mar. Admission costs $3 for kids and $4 for adults; skate rental costs $3.

Warren Park also has a **sledding hill**, **skateboard park**, and **tennis courts**, all of which are free.

▮▮▮▮ RESOURCES

DevonAvenue.com (www.devonavenue.com). It's the online portal for Chicago's Indo-Pak community. Get information on local restaurants and shops, as well as Bollywood gossip and cricket scores from the motherland.

4 • FAST BREAK: *Pilsen Sampler*

An afternoon spent munching in Pilsen? Que buen idea, amigo. Especially since one can visit a top-notch art museum, take a flamenco lesson, and purchase a life-altering candle there, too.

Pilsen is ground zero for Chicago's Mexican community. When you step onto 18th Street, the neighborhood's main vein, which is teeming with taquerias, street vendors, and shops selling soccer jerseys and Spanish-language books, it's easy to believe you're strolling far south of the border.

Beyond the *elotes* and *carnitas* to gorge on, Pilsen is a place to devour art. More than 30 storefront galleries and studios cluster around 18th and Halsted Streets. Bright murals cover the community's walls. And the National Museum of Mexican Art ensures visual arts remain at the neighborhood's forefront.

Pilsen has long been a port of entry for immigrants. In the late 1800s, Eastern Europeans flocked here to work in the factories and stockyards. It was the Czech contingent who dubbed the 'hood "Pilsen" after the town they pined for back in their Bohemian homeland. Upton Sinclair, author of *The Jungle*, wasn't so flattering. He referred to Pilsen as "that slum." By the 1970s, Mexicans had replaced Eastern Europeans as Pilsen's main immigrant source, and today the community of over 40,000 people is approximately 90 percent Mexican and Mexican American.

As you walk around, you'll notice many homes have their front yards several feet below sidewalk level, giving the place a sunken look. Residents can thank City Hall for the submersion, which took place more than a century ago. Workers at the time had to raise the streets for sewer construction, well after the old homes had been holding their ground.

Many Pilsen businesses close on Monday, but the rest of the week the neighborhood pulses with festive beats and bites—and the best chocolate cake you've ever laid lips on.

▪▪▪▪ GETTING THERE

Pilsen is a few miles southwest of downtown's Loop. Take the Pink Line train to 18th Street if you're coming via public transportation. By car, take I-90/94 to exit 52C for 18th Street. The exit merges onto South Union Avenue briefly until you reach a traffic light; turn right for 18th Street (and be aware that 18th is interrupted at Halsted Street, but it continues on the other side of Halsted to the north).

For parking, try Ashland Avenue, which is meter-free. Otherwise, load up on quarters to feed the hungry beasts on most other area roads.

▪▪▪▪ EATING OUT

True, you can nibble brain tacos and beef cheeks while in the neighborhood, but let's ease into the Pilsen food scene in a gentler fashion. The restaurants below provide an introduction to dishes you'll see on local menus, and we've provided rough translations of their Spanish names. The eateries are listed in order from west to east, in case you want to graze down 18th Street from the train station.

Street food: Umbrella'd food carts fill Pilsen's sidewalks, particularly around Harrison Park (1824 South Wood Street), tempting passersby with an array of snacks. Popular items include spicy-sweet *verduras* (thin slices of melon or cucumber dusted with a chili-powder kick) and *elotes* (an ear of corn slathered

with mayonnaise, crumbled Mexican cheese, and chili powder). Cold, pulpy *agua frescas* (fruit-flavored waters) refresh the taste buds and ready you for the next snack.

Nuevo Leon (312-421-1517), 1515 West 18th Street. Open daily 7 AM–12 AM. Nuevo Leon is the real enchilada, feeding hungry Pilsenites and visitors from around the city for more than four decades. The Gutierrez family steams, fries, grills, roasts, simmers, and stews traditional dishes for peso-size prices, and they aren't at all stingy when ladling out the goods. Kudos, in particular, to the homemade

One of many murals splashed across buildings on 18th Street, Pilsen's main commercial corridor

chorizo (sausage) and chicken smothered in chocolatey mole sauce. Nuevo Leon is a great option if you're looking for a big, color-splashed restaurant experience versus a hole-in-the-wall diner ambience. It's BYOB, which also helps keep the tab low. Cash only. Breakfast $3–5, dinner mains $10–15.

Restaurant La Casa Del Pueblo (312-421-4664), 1834 South Blue Island Avenue. Open daily 6 AM–8 PM. Multigenerational families swarm this cafeteria-style restaurant, next to a grocery store with the same name. Mom, dad, junior, and grandpa eyeball the homey dishes behind the counter, like *chilaquiles* (egg, tortilla strips, and chilies fried together), *tortas de camaron* (fried shrimp patties), and *pollo en salsa* (chicken breast cooked in a zucchini and corn stew), then carry their picks to the simple tables for a group feast. Mains, $6.35–8.

Don Pedro Carnitas (312-829-4757), 1113 West 18th Street. Open Mon. through Fri. 6 AM–6 PM, Sat. 5 AM–5 PM, Sun. 5 AM–3 PM. Look for the neon pink pigs in the window, and you've found Don Pedro's meat mecca. A machete-wielding gentleman greets you at the front counter, ready to hack off your pork pieces. He wraps the thick chunks with onion and cilantro into a fresh tortilla (the Del Ray factory is a few doors

down the road), and you take the taco to the no-frills tables in back and squeeze on lime juice and tomatillo salsa. Delicioso! The restaurant also serves *barbacoa* (meat traditionally slow-cooked in a pit), *birria* (spicy, slow-cooked goat stew), menudo (tripe and meat broth), and *chicharrones* (seasoned, deep-fried pork skin). Cash only. Tacos, $1.50.

Kristoffer's Cafe (312-829-4150), 1733 South Halsted Street. Open Mon. through Fri. 7:30 AM–9

A mural at the train station welcomes visitors to Pilsen.

Nuevo Leon has been dishing out traditional Mexican food for more than four decades.

PM, Sat. and Sun. 8 AM—8 PM. Is that a choir of angels singing, you wonder, as you sink your fork into Kristoffer's chocoflan? The creamy cake is that divine. Sometimes called *pastel imposible* (impossible cake), chocoflan mixes chocolate cake and flan (custard), and gets its name from the improbable baking process, whereby the cake starts at the bottom of the pan and the flan on top, but the two flip-flop while cooking in the oven. The café also makes traditional *tres leches* (three milks, a.k.a., condensed, evaporated, and regular) cakes, and serves a small menu of omelets, sandwiches, wraps, burritos, and tamales. Bright paintings by local artists cover the walls, and there's free wireless access for customers. Omelets and sandwiches, $4.50—6; cake slice, $4.50.

▪▪▪▪ WHAT TO SEE AND DO

Museum visiting: Be sure and stop into the **National Museum of Mexican Art** (312-738-1503; www.nationalmuseumofmexican art.org), 1852 West 19th Street. Open Tues. through Sun. 10 AM—5 PM. It's one of Chicago's best museums—and the largest Latino arts organization in the United States—though it's often overshadowed by the big-money institutes downtown. The works are all by Mexican artists, and the permanent collection includes classical paintings, shining gold altars, skeleton-rich folk art, beadwork, and exhibits on the Mexican Muralist Movement and Virgin of Guadalupe (a Mexican icon symbolizing hope and refuge). The museum also sponsors readings by top authors and performances by musicians and dance troupes. During the fall, the museum draws huge crowds for its exhibits and celebrations relating to the Day of the Dead (on November 1), a traditional Mexican holiday that combines the festive with the religious. The events take place for a month on either side of the holiday. And finally, don't leave without stopping in the museum's store, chock full of wildly colored Mexican handicrafts. Museum admission is free.

Mural ogling: Murals are a traditional Mexican art form, and they brighten buildings all over Pilsen. The genre is linked to the Mexican Revolution of 1910, when leaders used simple and expressive paintings to reach the people, many of whom were illiterate. Today inspired images grace Saint Pius Church (1919 South Ashland Avenue), painted with a mural of people eating corn while Jesus looks on. Another good example is the exterior wall of

Cooper Academy (1645 West 19th Street). It sports a sprawling mosaic with a diverse range of Mexican images, from a portrait of farmworker advocate Dolores Huerta to the Virgin of Guadalupe. Local artist Jose Guerrero leads **Pilsen Mural Tours** (773-342-4191), where you can learn more about the neighborhood's images; call to arrange an excursion. The 90-minute tours cost $100.

Gallery hopping: More than 30 galleries huddle near the intersection of Halsted and 18th Streets. A great time to come here is on Second Fridays (i.e., the second Fri. of each month, from 6 PM—10 PM), when all the galleries stay open late to welcome art aficionados with wine, snacks, and freshly hung paintings, ceramics, and photos. The **Chicago Arts District** (312-377-4444; www .chicagoartsdistrict.org) organizes the event and can provide further information. Intriguing stops include Vespine Gallery (1907 South Halsted Street, first floor), known for its papermaking; and 4Art (1932 South Halsted Street, #100), which specializes in large-scale group shows.

Candle shopping: Whether you're hoping to remove a jinx, fall in love, or win the lotto, there's a candle that can help at **Centro Botanico Guadalupano** (312-226-0106), 1538 West 18th Street. Open Mon. through Sat. 9

AM—7:30 PM, Sun. 9 AM—5:30 PM. Herbs, health remedies, incense, and religious icons also crowd the dusty shelves.

Flamenco dancing: Clap your hands and stamp your heels to the sultry beat at **Clinard Dance Theatre Studio** (312-399-1984; www.clinardance.org), 722 West 18th Street. Call for the lesson schedule. Cost for a five-week session (two classes per week) is $150, drop-in classes cost $20.

▪▪▪▪ SPECIAL EVENTS

The community's big holidays are **Cinco de Mayo** (May 5) and **Day of the Dead** (November 1). A parade marks the former, followed by a festival at Douglas Park (1401 South Sacramento Drive). Special foods, skeletons, and altars mark the latter, with the National Museum of Mexican Art leading the events. Early August's **Fiesta del Sol** (www.fiestadelsol.org) is another huge neighborhood bash, with carnival rides, live music, and traditional foods.

▪▪▪▪ RESOURCES

Chicago Arts District (312-377-4444; www.chicagoartsdistrict .org), 1821 South Halsted Street. The Web site provides information on Pilsen artists, galleries, and exhibitions. The office is open during Second Friday events from 6 PM—9 PM and provides maps of gallery locations.

5 • MADISON'S FOODIE FRENZY

With its crunchy-meets-cosmopolitan mix, Madison is a foodie dream town. Any gastronome worth his French gray sea salt has made the pilgrimage to the city's farmers' market. It's the nation's largest producer-only spread, where all goods—including the wide selection of gourmet cheeses—are handmade by the guy or gal who's selling them at the fold-out tables. Even Madison's drinks have gourmet appeal: many bars pour locally brewed ales, while cafés dispense fair-trade coffee.

But the town isn't stuck on local. The range of global eats is like a U.N. roll call: Nepali, Afghan, Lao, Jamaican, and on down the roster.

Madison racks up plenty of praise beyond its chow. It's lauded as one of the top green cities, the best road-biking town, the number-one walking city, a biotech hot spot, the nation's finest canoe town, and one of the top places "where dogs rule." Is there anything this fair city (population 223,000) can't do?

Apparently not, because it's also the Wisconsin state capital and host to the University of Wisconsin and its 42,000 students.

The town center rests on an isthmus bounded by lakes Monona and Mendota. State Street links the capitol to the university's expansive campus. The mile-long, pedestrian-only road is lined with feminist bookstores, parked bicycles, and stores selling Free Tibet stickers through clouds of jasmine incense. Several locavore and ethnic restaurants also fold into the scene. On the capitol's east side, Williamson Street is another food and drink gold mine; it's even more beatnik than State Street.

Madison is a winner to visit year-round. April through November offers the farmers' market, water sports, bike trails, and outdoor patios on which to imbibe. Winter is best spent in warm taverns and worldly museums admiring modern art and silent films. Epicurean eating goes on throughout the seasons.

▎▎▎▎ GETTING THERE

Madison is 150 miles northwest of Chicago. Take I-90/94 west out of Chicago; stay on I-90 west when it splits off. The interstate goes to Rockford, where it merges with I-39 and goes north. On the outskirts of Madison get onto US 18/12 west (a.k.a. The Beltline) for about 6 miles, and then look for the Park St. exit north into downtown. Parts of I-90 require tolls. The trip takes two and a half to three hours.

Public transportation is also an option. Climb aboard **Van Galder Bus** (800-747-0994; www.vangalderbus.com), which runs between Chicago (either O'Hare or downtown) and Madison's Memorial Union several times daily. The trip takes just over three hours and costs $27 one way. **Megabus** (877-462-6342; www.megabus.com/us) is quicker but less convenient location-wise. It runs two buses daily from downtown Chicago to Madison; drop-off is at Dutch Mill Park and Ride on the Beltline Highway, a fair distance from downtown (though accessible by city bus). The trip takes two and a half hours and costs $26 one way.

■■■■ GETTING AROUND

It's easy to get around the city center on foot. Bike rentals are another way to go (see What to See and Do, page 45). Metro Transit runs the public bus service. Cost is $1.50 per ride, $3.40 for a day pass.

■■■■ WHERE TO STAY

Arbor House (608-238-2981; www.arbor-house.com), 3402 Monroe Street. This mod, eight-room B&B wears its eco-heart on its sleeve. It uses wind power, energy-efficient appliances, natural-fiber sheets and towels, and all-natural cleaning prod-

Slow food pioneer L'Etoile Restaurant has been a foodie haven for more than 30 years

ucts. It's located about 3 miles southwest of the capitol but accessible to the public bus. Or use the house's free mountain bikes to get around; they're ideal for riding through the university's Arboretum across the street. Other perks include wireless access, a sauna, and free canoe passes. Rooms including vegetarian breakfast cost $110–175 on weekdays, $150–230 on weekends.

Best Western Inn on the Park (608-257-8811, 800-279-8811; www.innonthepark.net), 22 South Carroll Street. Since it's the only lodging on Capitol Square, the Inn on the Park does big business. The 212 rooms are clean and comfy, though a bit drab with their muted colors and dated furnishings. There's free parking and Internet access (wired in the rooms, wireless in the lobby), plus a restaurant and bar on-site. If you're coming for the farmers' market, it's at the hotel's doorstep. Rooms cost $135–185.

University Inn (608-285-8040, 800-279-4881; www.university inn.org), 441 North Frances Street. The good news first: the 45-room hotel is steps from State Street's action, it's low-priced, and has free parking and Internet access (wired in the rooms, wireless in the lobby). Now the bad news: it's loud and the decor is 1970s dumpy. Rooms cost $89–129.

▮▮▮▮ CAMPING

Capital Springs/Lake Farm Campground (608-575-5308, 608-224-3606; www.reservedane .com), Lake Farm Road (about 5 miles southeast of Capitol Square). Open Apr. 1 through Oct. 31. The modern campground has 54 sites (39 have electricity), with hot showers and flush toilets. It's located near the Capital City bike/hike trailhead (see What to See and Do, page 45). In fall, the campground fills with U of W Badger football fanatics, so make reservations (which must be done at least two weeks in advance). Campsites cost $16 per night, plus $7 for electricity.

▮▮▮▮ EATING OUT

Two excellent grazing areas are State Street and its environs around Capitol Square, and bohemian Williamson (a.k.a. Willy) Street, about a mile northeast of the square. Beer lovers should keep an eye out for local pours from Madison's own Capital Brewery, including year-round favorites Island Wheat, Munich Dark, and Special Pilsner.

Cafe Soleil and L'Etoile Restaurant (608-251-0500), 25 North Pinckney Street. Open Mon. through Sat. 7 AM–2:30 PM for the café; open Tues. through Thurs. 6 PM–8:30 PM, Fri. 5:30 PM–9:45 PM, and Sat. 5 PM—9:45 PM for the restaurant. Slow Food pioneer L'Etoile was serving "regionally reliant" cuisine long before everyone and their grandma went local. It has been sourcing meats, cheeses, and veggies from area producers since 1976. It's still a beloved foodie haven. The three-course prix fixe ($39) menu available Tues. through Thurs. is a good deal; a recent offering included chili-spiced shrimp bisque, pork shoulder tacos, and sweet corn crepes. Another thrill is the Wisconsin Artisan Cheese Tasting Plate, with 26 hunks of creamy goodness.

Soleil is the attached, sunny-yellow café, serving sandwiches like trout salad on fresh-baked honey-oat bread and Wisconsin grilled cheeses (a provolone, Swiss, and cheddar combo) on whole-grain bread. Don't leave without salivating over the case of French pastries; the Chocolate Sand Cookie (dark chocolate with sea salt) is the best seller. Café mains, $8—10; restaurant mains, $29—42.

Himal Chuli (608-251-9225), 318 State Street. Open Mon. through Sat. 11 AM—9 PM, Sun. 12 PM—8 PM. Mmm, Nepali food that gives "harmony and health through home-style cooking." Join professors, students, and trekker types sitting at the scat-tering of simple wood tables and conversing over steaming plates of momos (dumplings with peanut sauce), quati (winter soup made with nine kinds of beans), and other vegan and vegetarian dishes. Meat eaters, fear not: there's plenty for you, too, including chicken, lamb, beef, and bison in Nepali incar-nations. A short but sweet beer list (including local brews) adds to the pleasure. Cash only. Mains, $8—15.

Weary Traveler Free House (608-442-6207), 1201 Williamson Street. Open Mon. 4 PM—1 AM, Tues. through Sun. 11:30 AM—1 AM. Old-style speakeasy meets UK pub at the Weary Traveler. The low light-ing, dark wood decor, art-filled walls, and myriad board games complement the menu of global comfort foods. Top marks go to the Reuben sandwich, vegan chili, Hungarian goulash, and walleye sandwich with killer roasted potatoes. Everything on tap is local and/or craft brewed, including suds from Lake Louie (go with the Scotch Ale), Capital Brewery, and New Glarus. Mains, $7—11.

Memorial Union Terrace (608-265-3000), 800 Langdon Street, on the University of Wisconsin campus. Open Mon. through Thurs. 7 AM—9 PM, Fri. 7 AM—11 PM, Sat. 8 AM—12 AM, Sun. 11 AM—9 PM.

The uni's waterfront terrace is perfect for an outdoor drink, which explains why all of Madison is here gazing at Lake Mendota's sailboats on a nice day. In summer, there's often live music. Pub grub, $4.50—8.

Fresco (608-663-7374), 227 State Street, rooftop of the Museum of Contemporary Art. Open Tues. through Thurs. 5 PM—9 PM, Fri. and Sat. 5 PM—10 PM, Sun. 5 PM—9 PM. The triangular glass lounge is a swell place to sip a martini and admire the capital view. There's also a menu of contemporary American dishes. Mains, $15—28; martinis, $7.

▌▌▌▌ WHAT TO SEE AND DO

Foodie fun: The **Dane County Farmers' Market** (608-455-1999; www.dcfm.org) overtakes Capitol Square every Saturday from 6 AM— 2 PM from late April through early November. It's the country's largest producer-only market, which means the 150 vendors have personally grown or made the goods they're selling. Cheese and fresh vegetables are the most plentiful wares, but meats (bison and free-range emu, among others), flowers, maple syrup, and eggs are also on offer. Keep your eyes peeled for one man in particular: Willi Lehner of Bleu Mont Dairy, who makes fantastic

cheeses in his wind- and solar-powered cheese bunker, but in limited quantities. The farmers' market is your best chance to get your hands on his creations. Street musicians and arts and

Madison takes pride in its free trade coffee shops.

The Madison Museum of Contemporary Art offers Frida Kahlo and a rooftop martini bar.

crafts vendors add to the market's festival atmosphere.

Cheese shopping: If you miss the farmers' market and can't make it to Green County (see chapter 1), you can fill in the dairy gaps at **Fromagination** (608-255-2430; www.fromagination.com), 12 South Carroll Street. Open Mon. through Fri. 9 AM—6:30 PM, Sat. 7 AM—4 PM. It carries small-batch and hard-to-find local artisanal cheeses, as well as loads of information on wine and cheese (and beer and cheese) pairings. Dairy takes itself less seriously at the **House of Wisconsin Cheese** (608-255-5204; www.houseof wisconsincheese.com), 107 State Street. Open daily 9 AM—8 PM. It sells state-shaped cheddar blocks and foam rubber cheese-wedge hats among its flavorful stock.

Walking tours: Put on your walking shoes and set off with a guide from the **Madison Trust for Historic Preservation** (608-441-8864; www.madisontrust.org). Departure points vary. Most tours are held on Saturday mornings May through September. The group's six routes include State Street (which comes with the bonus of a free ice cream scoop at a local shop) and King Street (which explores the restaurant district and includes a free drink at a local pub). The hour-long tours are a steal at $5.

Biking: Madison proclaims it's the bike capital of the Midwest, and with 120 miles of trails and purportedly more bikes than cars on its roads, who's to argue? Rent wheels at **Budget Bicycle Center** (608-251-8413), 1230 Regent Street, about 1.5 miles from Capitol Square by the university. Open Mon. through Fri. 9 AM—9 PM, Sat. 9 AM—7 PM, Sun. 10 AM—7 PM. The shop is near trails that will take you straight downtown, to the arboretum (see page 47), or out to the **Capital City State Trail**, a 7-mile paved path that sweeps south of the Beltline Highway, along Lake Monona, and around to the convention center downtown. Riders do not have to pay the usual state trail fee to use this one. Hybrid bikes cost $20 per day.

Kayaking and canoeing: It'd be a shame to leave town without wetting a paddle in the city's lakes. **Rutabaga Paddlesports** (608-223-9300, 800-472-3353; www.rutabaga.com), 220 West Broadway (about 5 miles southeast of Capitol Square), sets you afloat from its store-side dock. Kayak/canoe rentals cost $25 for a half day, $40 for a full day.

Arts appreciation: Paintings by Frida Kahlo and Claes Oldenburg hang at the mod, glassy **Museum of Contemporary Art** (608-257-0158; www.mmoca

.org), 227 State Street. Open Tues. and Wed. 11 AM—5 PM, Thurs. and Fri. 11 AM—8 PM, Sat. 10 AM—8 PM, Sun. 12 PM—5 PM. The rooftop holds a sculpture garden, cinema that screens art films ($5 per person), and a stylish restaurant and martini lounge. Admission is free.

The museum is connected to the **Overture Center for the Arts** (608-258-4141; www.overture center.com), 201 State Street, which hosts jazz, classical, opera, dance, and world music performances.

Capitol building: The **Wisconsin State Capitol** (608-266-0382), surrounded by Carroll, Main, Pinckney, and Mifflin Streets, is the tallest dome outside Washington, D.C. It's open Mon. through Fri. 8 AM—6 PM, Sat. and Sun. 8 AM—4 PM, with tours usually available on the hour. Admission is free.

University of Wisconsin: The campus has its own attractions, including the **Memorial Union** (608-265-3000), 800 Langdon Street, with its lakeside terrace for outdoor drinking, people watching, boat rentals, and free live music and films. The **Babcock Hall Dairy Store** (608-262-3045), 1605 Linden Drive, sells student-made cheese and ice cream from the university's dairy plant. It's open Mon. through Fri. 9:30 AM—5:30 PM, Sat. 10 AM—1:30 PM. The

Chazen Museum of Art (608-263-2246; www.chazen.wisc.edu), 800 University Avenue, displays a quirky, epoch-spanning collection of paintings, sculptures, and decorative arts in 24,000 square feet of gallery space. It's open Tues. through Fri. 9 AM—5 PM, Sat. and Sun. 11 AM—5 PM. Hiking and biking trails zigzag through the lilac-strewn, 1,260-acre **Arboretum** (608-263-7888; www.uw arboretum.org), 1207 Seminole Highway. It's open daily 7 AM—10 PM. Volunteers lead free walks, often on Sundays; call for times. Admission is free to the university sites.

▪▪▪▪ DON'T FORGET

Bring a cooler to keep farmers' market purchases fresh during your drive home.

▪▪▪▪ SPECIAL EVENTS

Early August: Great Taste of the Midwest Beer Festival (www.mhtg .org). Around 120 craft brewers uncork their dark stouts, blueberry Lambics, and plum meads.

Late May: World's Largest Brat Fest (www.bratfest.com). More than 190,000 bratwursts go down the hatch annually at this family-focused fair with rides and live music over Memorial Day weekend.

Mid-October: Wisconsin Book Festival (www.wisconsinbook

festival.org). Venues around town host four days of big-name authors in fiction, nonfiction, poetry, and children's literature.

▌▌▌▌ NEARBY

Taliesin (608-588-7900, 877-588-7900; www.taliesin preservation.org), intersection of WI 23 and County Road C, 40 miles west of Madison and 3 miles south of Spring Green. Open daily 9 AM–5:30 PM May 1 through Oct. 31. Frank Lloyd Wright fans can make the pilgrimage to Taliesin, Wright's home for most of his life and the site of his architectural school. The house was built in 1903, the Hillside Home School in 1932, and the visitors center in 1953. Guided tours cover various parts of the complex; you'll need reservations for the more in-depth circuits. The one-hour Hillside Tour ($16, no reservation needed) is a good introduction. There's also a two-hour house tour, two-hour shuttle bus/walking tour, and four-hour estate tour. The Midwest's other big Wright shrine is in Oak Park, Illinois; see Chapter 11 for details. Taliesin tours cost $16–80.

For a map of more architectural sites near Taliesin, go to www .springgreen.com/architectural gems.asp. The noted **American Players Theatre** (608-588-2361; www.playinthewoods.org) is also in the area and stages classical productions at an outdoor amphitheater by the Wisconsin River.

▌▌▌▌ RESOURCES

Madison Convention and Visitors Bureau (608-255-2537, 800-373-6376; www.visitmadison .com), 615 East Washington Avenue (six blocks northeast of Capitol Square). Open Mon. through Fri. 8 AM–5 PM. Provides a useful Visitors Guide, town map, and even a downloadable Green Visitors Guide to help lighten your eco-footprint while in town.

Welcome Center (608-262-4636), 21 North Park Street. Open Mon. through Fri. 9 AM–4:30 PM, Sat. 11 AM–2 PM. Provides info on the city and university campus (for the latter, the Memorial Union also holds heaps of information).

Isthmus (www.thedailypage .com). Pick up this excellent free weekly alternative newspaper to help plan your weekend.

PLAY

6 • BEYOND THE DELLS' WATERPARKS

Everyone knows about the Wisconsin Dells—the "waterpark capital of the world," with 21 resorts to splish-splash in, water-skiing thrill shows, pirate-kitsch minigolf courses, and a slew of other carny attractions to wow families.

The Dells is a $1 billion tourism juggernaut, and it does a fine job telling visitors how to ride the Ducks, or see daredevils juggle chainsaws, or where to buy fudge and gumdrops downtown.

So we're taking this opportunity to focus on the Dells' lesser-known attractions, the ones that drew visitors here in the first place. Because before Believe It or Not shows took over the scene, families came to the Dells for a nature fix amid limestone gorges and rushing rivers.

You can still get a dose of these outdoor prizes at Mirror Lake and Devil's Lake, where water plus park equals something totally different than it does in the Dells proper. The two natural areas offer camping, hiking, and paddling that are among the Midwest's most scenic, and it's extraordinary that they exist side by side with the Dells' commercialism. The endangered whooping crane stalks the wetlands nearby, and birds of a different feather inhabit the psychedelic world at Dr. Evermor's sculpture park to the south.

Go ahead: give the Dells' flip side a try. Not only does it provide plenty of ways to play, but it often makes for a more economical getaway than the usual Dells doings.

▌▌▌▌ GETTING THERE

The Wisconsin Dells are 195 miles northwest of Chicago. Take I-90/94 west out of Chicago; stay on I-90 west when it splits off. The interstate goes to Rockford, then turns north for Wisconsin, and you'll have to fork over tolls en route. In Madison, I-90 rejoins I-94, and together they roll to the Dells. Exit 87 (for WI 13 north) will take you to the town center. The trip takes three to three and a half hours.

▌▌▌▌ GETTING AROUND

The Dells are divided into a north area and south area. US 12 connects them, and it's the road that holds the majority of attractions. It's also the main vein south to Mirror Lake (6 miles from the Dells' core), the crane foundation (9 miles), Baraboo (13 miles), Devil's Lake (18 miles), and Dr. Evermor's Sculpture Garden (21 miles). Madison lies about 55 miles south of the Dells.

A lot of traffic descends on US 12, and the highway can be jammed entering the Dells on Friday night.

▉▉▉▉ WHERE TO STAY

Rates at the resorts vary wildly. You can call, then try again five minutes later and get quoted an entirely different price. Try bargaining for your room. Tell the operator you were given a lower rate during an earlier call, and ask if there's any way to still get that price. (We had this scenario recently, and after consulting with a supervisor, the operator knocked $60 off the rate.) It works primarily for last-minute reservations.

Kalahari Waterpark Resort (877-525-2427; www.kalahari resorts.com), 1305 Kalahari Drive (South Dells). Yes, it's a 750-room water park resort. And yes, it's chaos with both families and conventioneers swamping the place. But the rooms are darn nice—with comfy beds, soft sheets, a small private deck, and free wireless access—and they can be good value with prices dropping as low as $99 per night. Alas, you will endure a jungle theme and a dinky bathroom. Rooms cost $99–219.

Black Hawk Motel (608-254-7770; www.blackhawkmotel .com), 720 Race Street (North Dells). Open mid-Apr. through late Oct. Black Hawk offers 75 clean, no-frills motel rooms with DVD players, free wireless access, mini-refrigerators, and micro-

▉▉▉▉ LAKE DELTON'S DISAPPEARANCE

Visitors see a lot of magic shows when they come to the Dells, but Lake Delton's disappearance wasn't part of the program. The man-made lake, home to various resorts and the Tommy Bartlett Water Show, vanished in June 2008 during a massive storm. The shore gave way, and all the water drained out and tumbled into the Wisconsin River below. Luckily no one was hurt. The town is refilling the lake, and it's set to reopen—complete with backflipping water-skiers—in spring 2009.

waves. Friendly staff keep the grounds, including indoor and outdoor pools and a playground, well-maintained. The property is four blocks from the Dells' downtown shopping and restaurant core. Rooms come in several shapes and sizes and cost $85–175.

■■■■ CAMPING

Mirror Lake and Devil's Lake both accept reservations (888-947-2757; www.reserveamerica.com) for a $10 fee. In summer, it's crucial to book ahead. Entry into the parks by car requires a vehicle permit, which costs $10/day or $35/year. Campsites cost $17, plus $5 for electricity.

Mirror Lake State Park (608-254-2333; www.mirrorlake wisconsin.com), E10320 Fern Dell Road (a half mile south of I-90/94 on US 12, then 1.5 miles west on Fern Dell Road). Open year-round. The park offers 150 sites spread across three campgrounds. Bluewater Bay is closest to the visitor center and amphitheater; Sandstone is closest to the beach and boat landing; and Cliffwood is the smallest of the three, located north of Sandstone. Each of the campgrounds has hot showers and flush toilets as well as pit toilets. Some sites have electricity.

Devil's Lake State Park (608-356-8301; www.devilslake wisconsin.com), S5975 Park Road (2 miles south of Baraboo on Highway 123). Open year-round. Devil's Lake also has three campgrounds, and these hold more than 400 campsites. Ice Age has no electric sites and is the most wooded venue; it has the park's lone grocery/supply store. Quartzite is more open and grassy, with both electric and

The Trojan Horse at Mt. Olympus Water & Theme Park is one of the Dells' kitschier sights.
PHOTOGRAPH BY LISA BERAN

Fudge and gum drops pave the streets in the Dells' downtown area.

nonelectric sites; it's where the majority of RVs stay. Northern Lights is in between; it's the oldest campground, with shower facilities built by the Civilian Conservation Corps in the 1930s. The campgrounds share 10 shower/restroom buildings.

■■■■ EATING OUT

It's almost impossible to find a nonoverpriced, standout meal.

Cheese Factory Restaurant (608-253-6065), 521 Wisconsin Dells Parkway (South Dells). Open Thurs. through Sat. 11 AM–9 PM, Sun. 9 AM–7:30 PM. Here's your exception to the cruddy food rule. The Cheese Factory serves a menu that's 100 percent vegetarian, and there are vegan, gluten-free, and organic options, too. Breakfast dishes include blueberry pancakes and soy sausage omelets; lunch could be quinoa salad or a charbroiled tofu sandwich; and dinner options range from beer cheese soup to pizzas to variations on global dishes like Thai stir-fry and Malaysian noodles. An old-time soda fountain and bakery provide satisfying desserts. And yes, the building used to house a cheese factory. Breakfast, $7–11; sandwiches, $9–11; mains, $7–14.

Denny's Diner (608-254-7647), 2 Munroe Street (at US 12 and WI 23, South Dells). Open daily 6:30 AM–1:30 PM. Nothing fancy here, just good ol' greasy spoon eggs, hash browns, and homemade cinnamon buns amid the to-be-expected Dells kitsch (Elvis statue! Pac-Man game!) and kids running wild. Mains, $4–8.

■■■■ WHAT TO SEE AND DO

The sights are listed in geographic order from the Dells (i.e., Vertical Illusions is closest, while Dr. Evermor's place is farthest).

Vertical Illusions (608-253-2500; www.verticalillusions.com), 1009 Stand Rock Road (just west of the Dells town center). This outdoor adventure center specializes in guided rock climbing excursions in the area, and kayak tours on the Wisconsin River—a fantastic way to experience the "real" Dells. It also rents bicycles, cross-country skis, and snowshoes. Two-hour tours cost $65 per person, four-hour tours cost $95.

Big Sky Twin Drive-In Theatres (608-254-8025; www.bigskydrivein.com), on WI 16 a few miles east of the Dells, screens two double features nightly in summer and on weekends in May and September. Bring lawn chairs and a portable radio (to play the sound), and you'll greatly enhance your viewing pleasure.

Tickets cost $8 for adults, $5 for children.

Mirror Lake State Park (608-254-2333; www.mirrorlake wisconsin.com), E10320 Fern Dell Road (a half mile south of I-90/94 on US 12, then 1.5 miles west on Fern Dell Road). Open year-round. Just 6 miles from the Dells' center, Mirror Lake is a whole other world. Tall sandstone bluffs surround the lake and keep it calm; this allows the clear reflections that prompted the park's name. More than 28 miles of hiking trails stripe the landscape, including the easy, 0.6-mile Echo Rock Trail with bluffs and lake views, and the hilly, 2.5-mile Northwest Loop Trail through rocky outcrops. Canoe, kayak, and bike rentals are available at the boat landing in summer, and there's a swimming beach nearby. In winter, cross-country skiers glide over 19 miles of groomed trails, and ice fisherfolk set up on the lake. Even architecture buffs get a thrill here: Frank Lloyd Wright's Seth Peterson Cottage is tucked in the woods, and visitors can rent it ($275 per night) if they get on the waiting list two years in advance. Or check it out via the open house ($2) held the second Sunday of every month. Admission to the park costs $10 per car. An annual pass costs $35 per car.

International Crane Foundation (608-356-9462; www.saving cranes.org), E11376 Shady Lane Road (a mile off US 12). Open daily 9 AM–5 PM mid-Apr. through late Oct. This is one of the few places in the world to see whooping cranes, of which there are only about 500 left in the world. The Foundation hatches their eggs here, and workers dress in crane outfits and teach the young whoopers how to fly using ultra-light planes. Fourteen other crane species also live on-site. The small education center tells their stories, and you can see the lanky creatures in action on the two-hour guided wetland tours at 10 AM, 1 PM, and 3 PM. Admission costs $8.50 for adults, $4 for children.

Circus World Museum (608-356-8341, 866-693-1500; www .wisconsinhistory.org/circus world), 550 Water Street (in Baraboo). Open daily 9 AM–6 PM mid-May through early Sept., reduced hours the rest of the year. Baraboo was once the winter home of the Ringling Brothers Circus. The museum preserves a nostalgic collection of antique wagons, posters, and memorabilia from the touring big-top heyday. In summer, admission includes clowns, elephants, camels, and acrobats performing in shows that are surefire kid-pleasers. The pretty Baraboo River runs through the middle of the museum's grounds, and a bridge connects the two sides. No matter where you are, you'll hear the incessant chirpy circus music that's piped in throughout. Admission costs $7 in winter and $15 in summer for adults; $3.50 in winter and $8 in summer for children.

Devil's Lake State Park (608-356-8301; www.devilslake wisconsin.com), S5975 Park Road (2 miles south of Baraboo on Highway 123). Open year-round. Devil's Lake is Wisconsin's busiest park, with more than one million visitors annually. Five-hundred-foot bluffs tower above a 360-acre lake formed by a meteor (according to Ho-Chunk legend).

Dr. Evermor creates whimsical art from scrap metal at his sculpture park.

Hikers swarm in to walk the 29 miles of trails. Balanced Rock and Devil's Doorway are popular paths that both lead to odd rock formations. The 0.8-mile Parfrey's Glen trek through a primeval rocky gorge is the best of the bunch; it's located about 4 miles east of the lake off Solum Lane from Hwy 113. Canoe rentals are available at the concession stand on the lake's north shore. The bluffs draw loads of rock climbers. And even if it's a freezing cold winter day, Devil's Lake has crowds cross-country skiing, sledding, and ice-fishing. Not feeling that active? You can always drop in to picnic—the lakefront grove was voted best picnic spot in the state. Three native burial mounds shaped like a lynx, bear, and bird dot the park; ask at the entrance for directions to them. Admission to the park costs $10 per car. An annual pass costs $35 per car.

Dr. Evermor's Sculpture Park is on US 12 a few miles south of Devil's Lake. Open Mon., Thurs., Fri., and Sat. 9 AM—5 PM, Sun. 12 PM—5 PM. Dr. Evermor—a.k.a. artist Tom Every—welds old pipes, carburetors, and other salvaged metal into a hallucinatory world of futuristic creatures and structures. The pièce de résistance is the giant, egg-domed Forevertron, cited by Guinness as the world's largest scrap-metal sculpture at one time. The doc claims the 300-ton piece will one day take him into outer space. He and/or his wife Eleanor are often around (look in the car or trailer) and happy to chat about the bizarre birds, dragons, chimes, and other pieces of folk art. Be aware the park's entrance can be tricky to find. Look for the Badger Army Ammunition Plant, and then for a small sign leading you into a driveway across the street from the plant. Admission is free.

▉▉▉▉ SPECIAL EVENTS

Early September: Annual Cow Chip Throw (www.wiscowchip .com), Prairie du Sac (about 27 miles south of the Dells). More than 800 competitors fling dried manure patties; the record is 248 feet.

Mid-October: Autumn Harvest Festival (www.dells.com/harvest fest.htm), Dells. Scarecrow stuffing, apple eating, pumpkin decorating, and a farmers' market, plus a microbrew taste fest on Saturday of the weekend-long shebang.

Mid-January: Flake Out Festival (www.dells.com/flakeout.htm), Dells. A chilly weekend of snow sculptures, snow angels, mitten football, and a Hostess Sno Ball eating contest.

▉▉▉▉ NEARBY

Reedsburg (www.reedsburg.org) is a quiet antique town about 15 miles west of the Dells. It's also the starting point for the **400 Trail** (www.400statetrail.org), a 22-mile hiking/biking path that runs along the Baraboo River through wetlands and farms to the town of Elroy. Flooding in 2008 damaged portions of the trail, so check the status before setting out.

▉▉▉▉ RESOURCES

Wisconsin Dells Visitor and Convention Bureau (800-223-3557; www.wisdells.com). 701 Superior Street. Open daily 8:30 AM—5 PM. Chock full of info. Pick up the Vacation Guide, coupons, and City Pass (see below).

  Wisconsin Dells City Pass (www.dellscitypass.com). This pass can provide substantial savings if you're going to do core Dells sights like Shipwreck Lagoon mini-golf, Mt. Olympus Waterpark, the Army Ducks, etc. It costs $70 and is good for three days.

7 • BEACHED IN SAUGATUCK

They call it a "drinking town with an art gallery problem." That's not printed on Saugatuck's welcome sign, of course, but locals proudly declare it. And it is apt for this town on Michigan's west coast that booms in summertime thanks to its shoreline beaches, piney breezes, and welcome one, welcome all mind-set.

The good times started in 1910, when the Ox-Bow art colony set up shop here. Saugatuck embraced the new residents and their different lifestyles—a huge difference from the surrounding towns, such as Holland and Grand Rapids, which were ultrareligious and conservative. Word spread about Saugatuck's tolerance and natural beauty, and more artists flocked in, along with a substantial gay and lesbian population. Today more than 200 sculptors, potters, and painters live in the area, which includes several additional towns connected by the Blue Star Highway.

Saugatuck (population 1,000) anchors the scene. It sits along the Kalamazoo River as it curls into Lake Michigan, and most of the action takes place within a couple of blocks of the busy waterfront. Boats bob in the harbor. Inland, schlocky fudge and knickknack shops share the sidewalk with real-deal art galleries on Water and Butler Streets. It's a curious mix, as is the crowd of ice-cream-licking families, yuppie boaters, and martini-drinking gay couples. But that's what gives the town its charm.

Douglas (population 1,200) is Saugatuck's twin city. It's a mile or so south, and the two places have sprawled into one—although Douglas maintains its own wee, three-block commercial corridor. Both towns remain blissfully free of generic chain businesses, with nary a McDonald's or Starbucks in sight.

South Haven (population 5,000) is less cosmopolitan and more beach-focused, with lighthouse-dotted piers to stroll and ice cream and cutesy shops to browse. And Fennville (population 1,400) is for foodies. It may be a farm town with a lone traffic light, but it's home to the most sophisticated fare around. Definitely pack an appetite and head inland to chow here.

Fruit orchards fill in the rest of the region. When visitors aren't at the beach, they're out picking fresh blueberries, raspberries, apples, and peaches. Watch for roadside stands. The growing season runs from June through October—which is Saugatuck's season in general. Between November and April, most businesses have limited hours and close midweek. Weekends can still be a good time, since prices plummet. The bold can cross-country ski or snowshoe. Those who prefer the indoors can brew their own beer, or just drink it.

▪▪▪▪ GETTING THERE

Saugatuck is 140 miles northeast of Chicago. Take I-90/94 east from downtown. Follow I-90 east when it splits off (around 63rd Street) toward Indiana. Stay on I-90 for roughly 30 miles; you'll pay about $5 in tolls along the way. Take exit 21 to merge onto I-94 east (toward Detroit), and stay on it for 65 miles. After Benton Harbor, take exit 34 to merge onto I-196/US 31 north. Stay on the road for about 40 miles, until you see exit 36 for Saugatuck/Douglas. From the exit, turn right onto the Blue Star Highway and it takes you into town. The trip takes about two and a half hours.

▪▪▪▪ GETTING AROUND

The Blue Star Highway connects Saugatuck/Douglas to the neighboring coastal towns of Glenn (9 miles south) and South Haven (18 miles south). Fennville is about 3 miles south of Saugatuck/Douglas on the Blue Star, and then 6 miles inland via MI 89.

Saugatuck's roads are narrow and crowded, and parking is limited. If you can't find a spot in the Culver Street lot as you enter town (costing $5 per day), head over to Saugatuck High School on Elizabeth Street. It's free to park there, and a free shuttle bus will take you downtown (or you can walk the half-mile distance).

▪▪▪▪ WHERE TO STAY

If you stay in Saugatuck proper you're where the action is, walkable to the galleries, restaurants, and boating/party scene. But you'll pay for the privilege. To save dough, snooze in slower-paced Douglas or Fennville, if you don't mind finagling for parking when you come into Saugatuck.

The area brims with B&Bs in its century-old Victorian homes. Prepare for a frilly onslaught of canopy beds, rose-splattered wallpaper, and candlelit breakfasts on doily-covered tables. Most B&Bs cost $150 to $300 per night in the summer high season.

The visitors bureau (269-857-1701; www.saugatuck.com) has a comprehensive list of B&Bs, motels, cottages, and rental properties. Almost all places have a two-night minimum stay on weekends.

Bayside Inn (269-857-4321; www.baysideinn.net), 618 Water Street, Saugatuck. This former boathouse on Saugatuck's waterfront is a great option. The 10 rooms all have private balconies, wireless Internet, and access to the outdoor hot tub. Rooms including full breakfast cost $110–265.

Ship 'N Shore Motel/Boatel (269-857-2194; www.shipnshore motel.com), 528 Water Street, Saugatuck. Ship 'N Shore has the best location of all. It spreads along the waterfront right in downtown Saugatuck, and

boaters can tie up their vessels in the berths out front. The 40 rooms are nothing special, but the grounds are, which is why the place is often booked full with a classy clientele. Amenities include an outdoor pool, Jacuzzi, and wireless access. Rooms including continental breakfast cost $165–175 on weekends, about $30 less on weekdays.

Pines Motorlodge (269-857-5211; www.thepinesmotorlodge .com), 56 Blue Star Highway, Douglas. They aren't kidding about the pine at this fun-loving classic motel—not only is it surrounded by tall fragrant evergreens, but the beds, dressers, ceiling, and window frames are all carved from the wood. Retro tiki lamps, a mini refrigerator, microwave, and wireless Internet access round out the interior, and each room has Adirondack chairs

The Pines Motorlodge provides comfy seats where you can sit and watch the stars pop out.

outside where you can sit to watch the evening stars pop out. Prices include continental breakfast daily in July and August, and weekends in spring and fall. Rooms cost around $129.

Douglas House B&B (269-857-1119; www.douglashouseinn.com), 41 North Spring Street, Douglas. This four-room B&B is unique in many ways. First, there's no minimum stay. Second, it's not out-of-control flouncy. And third, you must pay by cash or check. Free bike use and wireless Internet access add to the deal. Rooms including continental breakfast cost $99 on weekdays, $130–150 on weekends.

▮▮▮▮ CAMPING

Holland State Park (616-399-9390; www.michigandnr.com /parksandtrails), 2215 Ottawa Beach Road, Holland (17 miles north of Saugatuck). Open Apr. through Oct. The wide, sandy beach at Holland makes it one of Michigan's most popular parks. There are two campgrounds: one at Lake Macatawa, with 211 sites; and the other adjacent to the beach day-use area on Lake Michigan, with 98 sites. Both sport modern facilities, including showers, flush toilets, and electricity; there's even wireless access by the beach ($4 per day) and a handy store nearby.

Reserve (800-447-2757; www .midnrreservations.com) well in advance. Visitors arriving by car must have a vehicle permit, which costs $8/ day or $29/year. Campsites cost $27 per night, plus an $8 reservation fee.

▮▮▮▮ EATING OUT

Journeyman Cafe/Rye Public House (269-561-2269), 114 East Main Street, Fennville. Open Wed. through Sun. 9 AM–10 PM. Foodies swoon over the organic, locally sourced ingredients that chef Matt Millar transforms into exquisite dishes. Simple yet classy, with exposed brick walls and natural wood tables, the space is actually two restaurants in one. Journeyman is inside the main entrance and has a higher-end menu with dishes such as wood-roasted halibut and grilled lamb loin over risotto. Rye is next door and offers a more informal menu of pizzas, sandwiches, and stews. But it doesn't matter where you sit—you'll be given both menus to choose from, and it's all fantastic. Shout-outs go to the brick-oven, thin-crust pizzas (sauced with, say, walnut pesto or olive tapenade) and the fat, crusty breads. Local wines and beers, along with outstanding international sips, help wash it all down. Intelligentsia coffee provides the morning caffeine

jolt. Breakfast, $6—12; lunch mains, $8—19; pizza, $13—17; dinner mains, $23—26.

Crane's Pie Pantry (269-561-2297), 6054 124th Avenue, Fennville. Open Mon. through Sat. 9 AM—8 PM, Sun. 11 AM—8 PM May 1 through Oct. 31, reduced hours Nov. 1 through Apr. 30. Ah, pie as it should be: not gloopy or overly sweet, just fresh fruit treated right and cradled by a light crust. Fruit orchards fan out behind the building and are where the peaches, apples, cherries, and other fillings come from. An old-fashioned, kitschy restaurant is on-site, too. Pies $3.75 per slice, $13 per whole.

Mermaid Bar and Grill (269-857-8208), 340 Water Street, Saugatuck. Open Sun. through Thurs. 11:30 AM—9:30 PM, Fri. and Sat. 11:30 AM—10:30 PM. The Mermaid packs 'em in on its outdoor patio overlooking the harbor. It serves a range of standards, from burgers to pasta to seafood dishes, but it's the water's-edge ambiance that makes it a hot spot. You can sit out here and just have a drink during nonrush times. Dinner mains, $11—22.

Saugatuck Brewing Company (269-857-7222), 2948 Blue Star Highway, Douglas. Open Sun. through Thurs. 11 AM—11 PM, Fri. and Sat. 11 AM—12 AM. Join the locals swillin' and chillin' at this microbrewery, which channels a community-center-meets-Irish-pub vibe. There are no TVs, no loud music, and no booze other than the slurpable suds made behind the bar. Beers range from the Oval Beach Blond Ale to the dark Boathouse Stout; samplers are available. There's live music on some nights, and a small menu of sandwiches served with tasty kettle chips. The kitchen closes at 10 PM. The brewery also offers beer-making classes (see What to See and Do, page 62). Sandwiches, $6.75—7.50.

Sherman's Dairy Bar (269-637-8251), 1601 Phoenix Road, South Haven. Open Mon. through

Sat. II AM—II PM, Sun. I2 PM—II PM
Mar. I through Oct. 31. Sherman's
ice cream comes in 50 flavors and
meal-size portions (don't be
fooled by the "baby" cone). The
goods can't get any fresher, since
they're whipped up in the on-site
factory. Lines snake out the door
on most days; take a number
from the counter inside. Single-
dip cones, $2.50—3.

▌▌▌▌ WHAT TO SEE AND DO

Beaches: They don't call the area
Michigan's Gold Coast for nothing. **Oval Beach** in Saugatuck
wins the popularity contest. Lifeguards patrol the long expanse of
fine sand, and there are bathrooms and concession stands,
though not enough to spoil the
peaceful, dune-laden scene. It
costs $5 to park (free after 6 PM,
which is convenient for sunset
gazing). Or you can walk from
the chain ferry; it's about I mile.

Douglas Beach looks like Oval's
poor relation. It's smaller, with
no lifeguards or concessions—but
no crowds, either.

South Haven's public beaches
may be the best of all. The two
main ones—**North Beach** and
South Beach—are downtown
flanking the boat-filled Black
River. Both are wide, with piers
jutting into Lake Michigan that
people stroll on and fish from.

South Beach's pier even has a
lighthouse. Both beaches are fully
loaded with concession stands,
bathrooms, volleyball nets, and
crowds. Water Street leads down
to the scene, and it, too, is
jammed with ice cream parlors,
fish restaurants, and family-
friendly shops. Parking costs $5.

Saugatuck Chain Ferry: This
little boat—the last of its kind on
the Great Lakes—is too cool. The
operator cranks the handle, and a
clackety chain unfurls behind the
vessel as it moves across the
Kalamazoo River. The ferry sails
from downtown Saugatuck (at
the foot of Mary Street) to Park
Street near Mt. Baldhead (about a
5-minute walk to the left of the
ferry dock). The crossing takes 5
minutes, and the operator often
lets guests—especially kids—do
the cranking. It runs from Memorial Day to Labor Day. A one-way
ride costs $I.

Mt. Baldhead: Huff and puff
up 282 stairs to get to the top of
this 200-foot-high sand dune,
and see Saugatuck and the Kalamazoo River spread out below.
You can race down the dune's
other side to Oval Beach, but
know this: the return slog up the
sand is hell.

Dune rides: Take a fun spin
though the sand with **Saugatuck
Dune Rides** (269-857-2253; www
.saugatuckduneride.com), 6495

▪▪▪▪ 'TIS THE SEASON

It's impossible to hold Mother Nature to an exact schedule, but in general the best pickin' times are:

Strawberries: June

Cherries: early July

Blueberries: July and August

Raspberries: July and August

Peaches: early August

Apples: September and October

Blue Star Highway. Open daily May to September. The 35-minute tour costs $16 for adults, $10 for children.

Gallery hopping/antique shopping: Galleries of pottery, paintings, sculptures, and glass-work flourish in downtown Saugatuck along Water and Butler Streets. Outside of town, antique shops dot the Blue Star Highway en route to South Haven. Often these places look like just a bunch of stuff in someone's front yard. But pull up in the right place at the right time, and that old traffic light or china teacup can be yours for a song.

Art-making: **Ox-Bow School of Art** (800-318-3019; www.ox -bow.org), 3435 Rupprecht Way, Saugatuck, offers classes June through October. Ox-Bow is affiliated with the School of the Art Institute of Chicago and offers instruction for both beginners and experienced artists ranging from single-session workshops to one- and two-week courses.

Mediums include ceramics, glass, painting, papermaking, print, and metals. To reach the forested grounds, take the road past Mt. Baldhead.

Fruit picking: Blueberries are king, but plenty of other fruits grow here, too. Pluck them yourself or buy them prepicked at the myriad roadside orchards. **Crane's U-Pick** (269-561-5126; www.cranesupick.com) is an offshoot of the pie place (see Eating Out, page 61), good for raspberries, apples, and peaches. **Earl's Farm Market** (269-227-2074; www.earlsberries.com) is on the Blue Star Highway 1 mile north of Glenn. It grows blueberries, strawberries, and raspberries. And **DeGrandchamp's** (269-637-3915; www.degrandchamps.com), 76241 14th Avenue in South Haven, grows blueberries only. It's also a nursery, so you can buy your own blueberry bush to plant at home. U-pick costs are usually around $1.50 per pound for blueberries, $2.50 for raspberries.

Beer brewing: Create your own suds at **Saugatuck Brewing Company** (269-857-7222; www.sbrewing.com), 2948 Blue Star Highway, Douglas. Brewmaster Barry Johnson will walk you through the process in three to four hours. You'll have to return in two weeks to bottle it. The payoff is 11 gallons of foamy goodness (a.k.a. sixty 22-oz bottles). Sessions take place on Saturday mornings. It costs $250, including all instruction, ingredients, and bottles, and it's fine to have up to four people as part of a group.

Biking: The **Kal-Haven Trail** (www.kalhaventrail.org) is a 34-mile crushed limestone path through woods, farms, and streams between South Haven and Kalamazoo. The trailhead is near the intersection of the Blue Star Highway and Wells Street in South Haven. Trail passes cost $3 per day, $15 per year.

Winter activities: Rent cross-country skis or snowshoes at **Landshark's** (269-857-8831; www.saugatucklandsharks.com), 306 Butler Street. Strap them on at nearby Saugatuck Dunes State Park and crunch through the woods to the lake. Equipment costs $14 per day.

■■■■ DON'T FORGET

Michigan is on eastern time, one hour ahead of Chicago.

■■■■ SPECIAL EVENTS

Mid-June: Waterfront Film Festival (www.waterfrontfilm.org), Saugatuck. They call it "the Sundance of the Midwest."

Late July: Venetian Festival (www.saugatuckvenetianfestival.com), Saugatuck. Decorated boats parade along the waterfront, followed by fireworks.

Mid-August: National Blueberry Festival (www.blueberryfestival.com), South Haven. Four days of pancake breakfasts, live music, sand castle—building, and a Blueberry Queen contest.

■■■■ NEARBY

The town of **Holland** (800-506-1299; www.holland.org), 12 miles north of Saugatuck, takes its Dutch heritage seriously and gives visitors all the windmills, wooden shoes, and tulips they can handle. Popular beachside Holland State Park lies a few miles outside of town.

Kalamazoo may not push your excitement button, but **Bell's Brewery** (269-382-2332; www.bellsbeer.com) will. Chicagoans suffered from withdrawal when Bell's beers were yanked from Illinois shelves between 2006 and 2008. They're back now, but why not drop by the source to see how they're made and stock up? Bell's Eccentric Cafe pours the classics, such as Amber Ale, Two Hearted Ale, and summery Oberon, as well as small-batch brews not distributed outside the pub. Kalamazoo is 37 miles inland from South Haven on MI 43, or you can bike the distance on the Kal-Haven Trail (see What to See and Do, page 64).

▌▌▌▌ RESOURCES

Saugatuck/Douglas Convention and Visitors Bureau (269-857-1701; www.saugatuck.com).

South Haven Visitors Bureau (800-764-2836; www.southhaven.org).

Gay Guide (www.gaysaugatuck douglas.com). Lists supportive area businesses. Available online or as a hard-copy booklet.

8 • SURFING THROUGH HARBOR COUNTRY

Sure, folks in Harbor Country discuss antique tables and ice cream flavors, like any other quaint Midwestern township. But interspersed with chats of estates sales and Chocolate Malt Supreme, locals also debate the merits of a quality wave, 2-millimeter-head booty, and the new pivot flex fin.

Harbor Country takes the area's rustic country charm and kicks it up a notch with surfing. You heard right. And you can share the stoke by taking lessons with dudes who drive a VW bus.

Let's back up a moment. Harbor Country is the collective name of eight small towns just over the Michigan border, stretching for 15 miles along Lake Michigan's shore. The area was popular in the 1920s and 1930s for Chicagoans escaping the city's summer heat. It fell out of favor until a couple of decades ago, when many urbanites fixed up second homes here.

From south to north, the towns are: Michiana and Grand Beach (where Mayor Daley has a pad), both mostly residential. New Buf-

falo is the largest Harbor community, home to the Third Coast Surf Shop, a booming public beach, ice cream shops, resorts, a boat-logged marina, and a popular farmers' market. The town of Three Oaks is the only Harbor community that's inland. It's a funky combination of farm hamlet and avant-garde art village, where you can pick up animal feed by the town square's gazebo, then walk over to the movie theater for a French New Wave film.

Union Pier, Lakeside, Harbert, and Sawyer are next in line. They're more prototypically "rustic" and "charming" with historic inns and B&Bs, antique shops, and galleries. Several wineries surround the communities and offer tastings. Warren Dunes State Park caps the scene. Its beach—perfect for lounging—and 240-foot dunes are a fine topper to a Harbor Country getaway.

The Red Arrow Highway connects the communities and parallels I-94. Summer is the busiest season, but fall is also popular as the trees burst into color. And hard-core surfers? Winter is your time, so bundle into your wetsuit and let the frontside carving commence.

■ ■ ■ ■ GETTING THERE

New Buffalo is 75 miles east of Chicago. Take I-90/94 east from downtown. Follow I-90 east when it splits off (around 63rd Street) toward Indiana. Stay on I-90 for roughly 30 miles; you'll pay about $5 in tolls along the way. Take exit 21 to merge onto I-94 east (toward Detroit), and stay on it for another 30 miles. After crossing the Michigan border, take exit 1 for New Buffalo and go left on LaPorte Road into town. The trip takes 90 minutes.

Three Oaks' old Featherbone Factory holds a hip theater and antique/garden store.

■ ■ ■ ■ GETTING AROUND

The Red Arrow Highway connects New Buffalo to the neighboring coastal towns of Union Pier, Lakeside, Harbert, and Sawyer; the distance between New Buffalo and Sawyer is 10 miles. Three Oaks, the only inland town, is 6 miles east of New Buffalo via US 12.

You'll need a car to get from town to town. Within towns, you often can find street parking and explore the town core on foot.

■ ■ ■ ■ WHERE TO STAY

The visitor bureau Web site (www .harborcountry.org/availability) provides contact info and descriptions of properties including B&Bs, inns, hotels, cottages, and campgrounds. It lets you search by price, pet-friendliness, and other categories. Many properties have a two-night minimum stay requirement.

Rabbit Run Inn (269-405-1050; www.rabbitruninn.com), 6227 Elm Drive, Sawyer. This four-room B&B opened in 2008. It sticks to an eco-agenda, using geothermal heating and air-conditioning, as well as enviro-friendly linens and cleaning supplies. Each room comes with a small refrigerator stocked with local fruits, cheese, and a bottle of wine from nearby Tabor Hill. Breakfast consists of fresh scones and muffins delivered to your door. Rooms have wireless access and a private deck. The owners provide guests with free bikes, beach chairs, and beach umbrellas. Rooms including breakfast cost $190–210 on summer weekdays, $215–235 on summer weekends (knock off $35 for winter rates).

Harbor Grand Hotel (888-605-6800; www.harborgrand.com), 111 West Water Street, New Buffalo. If you want to park the car and not move it, this 55-room waterfront property is a good choice since the public beach, restaurants, and wine shops are walking distance out the front door. Free bikes are also available for guest use. Inside it's all about comfy beds, breakfast in bed (delivered in a basket), and DVD watching with free rentals from the front desk. King rooms add a fireplace and Jacuzzi tub. Rooms including breakfast cost $209–300 in summer, and can drop as low as $119 in winter.

Holiday Inn Express (269-469-1400; www.ichotelsgroup.com), 11500 Holiday Drive, New Buffalo. This Holiday Inn Express wins high praise in the chain category. Lots of casino-goers stay here since it's just 2 miles from Four Winds Casino. It offers a free hot breakfast buffet every morning, and there's a small indoor pool. Rooms including breakfast cost $123–200.

Lakeside Inn (269-469-0600; www.lakesideinns.com), 15251 Lakeshore Road, Lakeside. Thirty-one rooms spread over three floors at this historic 1920s lodge. The rustic common areas sport mounted animal heads on the walls, a stone fireplace in the lobby, and front porch with rocking chairs. The rooms are nothing fancy, with plain, somewhat faded wood and wicker furnishings, but the private beach wins big bonus points. There's a café on-site and wireless access in the lobby. Rooms cost $115–200 in summer, $90–175 in winter.

▨▨▨▨ CAMPING

Warren Dunes State Park (269-426-4013; www.michigandnr.com/parksandtrails), 12032 Red Arrow Highway, Sawyer. Open Apr. through Oct. With 3 miles of beachfront, 6 miles of hiking and cross-country skiing trails, and climbable dunes that rise 260 feet in the air, visitors are all over this park in summer. There are two campgrounds: a modern one with 182 sites, 50-amp electrical hookups, hot showers, and flush toilets; and a rustic campground a quarter mile away with 36 sites and pit toilets. The modern area has lost much of its leafiness since the park had to remove 4,000 ash trees that were infested with beetles. Still, the campgrounds are packed and you'll need to reserve (800-447-2757; www.midnrreservations.com) in advance. Visitors arriving by car must have a vehicle permit, which costs $8/day or $29/year. Modern campsites cost $27 per night, rustic sites cost $16, and there's an $8 reservation fee.

▪▪▪▪ EATING OUT

Redamak's (269-469-4522), 616 East Buffalo Street, New Buffalo. Open daily 12 PM—10:30 PM, closed Nov. through Feb. Your arteries may suffer, but your taste buds will rejoice at the deep-fried and meaty selection at this old roadhouse with pinewood floors and Philips 66 gas pumps. Nothing beats a cheeseburger, spicy curly fries, and cold beer after a hard day of beach lounging. Cash only. Burgers and sandwiches, $4.50—9.

Blue Plate Cafe (269-469-2370), 15288 Red Arrow Highway, Union Pier. Open Mon. through Sat. 8 AM—3 PM, Sun. 9 AM—2 PM, closed Tues. and Wed. in winter. Colorful and cute, Blue Plate hits the tables with pancakes, omelets, and organic coffee for breakfast and thick panini sandwiches and salads for lunch. Staff offers samples of muffins and cookies from the house bakery while you wait. Cash only. Mains, $5—10.

Cafe Gulistan (269-469-6779),

13581 Red Arrow Highway, Harbert. Open Mon., Wed., and Thurs. 4 PM—10 PM, Fri. through Sun. 3 PM—11 PM, closed Tues. This squat, unassuming little building holds a Turkish restaurant that's one of the area's few ethnic eats. Turkish and Mediterranean standbys fill plates. Vegetarians can choose from smoky baba ganouj, crisp falafel in a garlic yogurt sauce, and salads with spicy roasted tomato or tangy cabbage and beets. Meat eaters can carve into lamb and chicken dishes. Beer and wine are on hand to support your order. At press time, Gulistan's owner, Ibrahim Parlak, was making headlines since the government has been trying to deport him—while the local community has been rallying around him—based on long-ago political affiliations in Turkey, so it's possible the restaurant will have a new owner by the time you're reading this. Mains, $8—14.

Luisa's Cafe (269-469-9037), 13698 Red Arrow Highway, Harbert. Open Wed. through Mon. 8 AM—3 PM, closed Tues., reduced hours in winter. Luisa's whips up breakfast and lunch items like Swedish pancakes, organic salads, and sandwiches with fresh-baked bread. Shout-outs go to the crab cake salad and spinach and goat cheese omelet. The café links to the Harbert Swedish Bakery. Cash only. Mains, $5—9.

Oink's Dutch Treat (269-469-3535), 227 West Buffalo Street, New Buffalo. Open Sun. through Thurs. 11:30 AM—10 PM, Fri. and Sat. 11:30 AM—11 PM. Ahh, 55 flavors of Sherman's Ice Cream are right here in case you can't make it to the source in South Haven (see chapter 7). Oink's interior is filled with pig-themed kitsch and kiddies dribbling the neon blue flavor. It's a few blocks inland from the beach. Cones cost $3—6.

■ ■ ■ ■ WHAT TO SEE AND DO

Beaches: Families swarm **New Buffalo Public Beach** and no wonder: it's wide and sandy, with big blue-green waves rolling in. Squint and you can almost imagine you're in Florida. Amenities include a snack shop and a bathhouse with outdoor shower. Lifeguards patrol during summer peak periods (they're off-duty during various weekdays). Rip currents are an issue here, so be careful and heed the posted warnings. Parking costs $2 per hour, or $10 per day in the public lot.

The other winner for sand-lounging is **Warren Dunes Beach** in the state park (see Camping, page 68) at 12032 Red Arrow Highway, Sawyer. A concession stand offers food, soft drinks, ice cream, and souvenirs from May through September. Parking is free in the big lot, but you'll need a state park vehicle permit to enter the grounds, which costs $8/day or $29/year.

Surfing: Amazing but true: you can surf Lake Michigan. Learn how with **Third Coast Surf Shop** (269-932-4575; www.thirdcoast surfshop.com), 22 South Smith Street, New Buffalo. Open daily 11 AM—6 PM in summer, reduced hours the rest of the year. The shop rents wetsuits and boards for surfing, paddleboarding, sandboarding, and skimboarding. For novices, they offer hour-and-a-half surfing lessons right from the public beach Thursday through Sunday from June through September. It's a great place to learn since the waves are gentle in summer (though big enough to be a thrill). Adding to the effect: the shop transports your equipment via an orange VW bus. All lessons must be reserved in advance. Board rentals cost $15/25 per half/full day. Wetsuits cost $10/15 per half/full day. Lessons (equipment included) cost $45/65 for group/private instruction.

Kayaking: Third Coast Surf Shop (see above) also rents kayaks and offers kayaking tours. For the **Galien River Tour**, the shop transports the vessels to a drop-off point 2 miles north of New Buffalo, and you paddle down the lazily flowing river to New Buffalo Public Beach, where the shop picks you up when you're finished. The trip takes two hours and costs $45 per kayak. If you want to rent a kayak sans tour and transportation, it costs $30/35 per half/full day.

Gaming: Woodsy lodge meets marble-and-granite flashiness at gargantuan **Four Winds Casino and Resort** (866-494-6371; www .fourwindscasino.com), 11111 Wilson Road, New Buffalo (about 3 miles east of town). Open daily 24 hours. If this baby was on the Vegas Strip it would be its second-largest casino. Four Winds ka-chings with 3,000 slot machines, 100 tables, and 2,500 employees. New Buffalo itself has only about 2,400 year-round residents, so you can see why they worried about the casino's impact when it opened in 2007. So far, the arrangement has gone smoothly. Four Winds is owned by the Poka-gon band of Potawatomi Indians.

Biking: Rent bikes at **Dewey Cannon Trading Company** (269-756-3361), 3 Dewey Cannon Avenue, Three Oaks. Open Sun. through Fri. 10 AM–4 PM, Sat. 10 AM–9 PM. The shop is Harbor Country's heart and soul for cyclists. Here you get the invaluable **Backroads Bikeway Map**, plotting out 14 routes from 5 to 60 miles on lightly used country roads. The routes start right out Dewey's front door. Cyclists with stamina like the 50-mile, mostly flat Grand Mere Trail that loops through orchards, lakefront parks, and the Tabor Hill vineyard, among others. Dewey also rents trailers for kids. Bikes cost $5 for the first hour, $2 per hour thereafter, or $15 per day.

Gallery hopping/antique shopping: Three Oaks is the artiest of the bunch and offers the **Third Saturday Gallery Walk**, when merchants stay open to 11 PM and host receptions, art demonstrations, and live music. The town's **Featherbone Factory** (269-756-7320), 111 North Elm

Lightly used country roads around Three Oaks are well-marked for biking.

Believe it: You can surf on Lake Michigan, and Third Coast Surf Shop will teach you how.

Street, holds a massive garden/ antique store with pottery, weather vanes, hand-carved cedar log furniture, and thousands of concrete garden stones made on-site. It's open Mon. through Sat. 10 AM—6 PM, Sun. 1 PM—5 PM, from Apr. through Oct. **Lakeside Antiques** (269-469-7717), 14876 Red Arrow Highway in Lakeside, and **Dunes Antique Center** (269-426-4043), 12825 Red Arrow Highway in Sawyer, provide fertile browsing grounds year-round. Dunes is the larger store and is good for buying used bikes.

Theater: As with galleries, Three Oaks flexes the region's strongest credentials for theater. The **Acorn Theater** (269-756-3879; www.acorntheater.com), 107 Generations Drive, is a nationally lauded, 250-seat avant-garde performance space carved out of a former corset-stay factory (a.k.a. the Featherbone Factory, which also holds the garden/ antique store listed above). Anything goes here—Shakespearean interpretations, kids' plays, opera, folk, jazz, and rock concerts, even recitals on the theater's pipe organ. The wine shop inside sells local wines and beers; it's open Friday through Sunday. A few steps away is the **Vickers Theatre** (269-756-3522; www .vickerstheatre.com), 6 North Elm

Street. Once the town's opera house, it has been beautifully restored into an art-house cinema that screens indie flicks. Acorn tickets cost around $10—20, Vickers tickets cost $8.

Winery tours: Wine is a major commodity in the area, and 10,000 acres of grapes blanket local land. The **Lake Michigan Shore Wine Trail** (www.miwine trail.com) provides a downloadable map of vineyards and tasting rooms. Most vineyards are signposted off the Red Arrow Highway and typically lie inland 6 miles or so. Tasting rooms pop up closer to the highway; Union Pier has a couple of tasting rooms in its town center. Admission is free to all venues.

Tabor Hill Winery (800-283-3363; www.taborhill.com), 185 Mt. Tabor Road, Buchanan, is widely regarded as the region's top winemaker. It offers tours daily every half hour from 12 PM— 4:30 PM May through Oct., and weekends only Nov. through Apr. Skip the restaurant and save your dough for bottles like the lush 2006 Lake Michigan Shore Cabernet Franc or a high-end sparkling wine.

Near Tabor Hill is **Round Barn Winery** (800-716-9463; www .roundbarnwinery.com), 10983 Hills Road, Baroda, with a café (serving lunch Fri. through Tues.

May through Oct.), so-so wines, and the intriguing DiVine Vodka, which they produce with grapes to fine results. Round Barn's tasting room is open Mon. through Sat. II AM—6 PM, Sun. I2 PM—6 PM.

Also in the 'hood is **Hickory Creek Winery** (269-422-1100; www .hickorycreekwinery.com), 750 Browntown Road, Buchanan. It's open Mon. through Sat. II AM—6 PM, Sun. I2 PM—6 PM. It makes a nice Riesling and also a slightly creamy and toasty 2005 chardonnay.

Meat grinding: It's not every day one gets to visit a butcher shop that has been around since Civil War days. **Drier's Meat Market** (888-521-3999), I4 South Elm Street, Three Oaks, is a historic site with antique grinders and cleavers, as well as famous smoked meats. It's open Mon. through Sat. 9 AM—5 PM, Sun. II AM—5 PM, closed Jan. through mid-Mar.

▪▪▪▪ SPECIAL EVENTS

Mid-June: Flag Day Celebration (www.30aks.org), Three Oaks. Beer, brats, games, and a rodeo surround the world's largest Flag Day parade.

Mid-August: Ship and Shore Festival (www.newbuffalo.com), New Buffalo. The weekend-long party offers art, food, live music, and surfing demonstrations and culminates with a lighted boat parade through the harbor.

Late September: Apple Cider Century (www.applecidercentury .com), Three Oaks. Seven thousand riders converge for this one-day bicycle tour through the area's orchards, forests, and wine country; riders choose the 25-, 50-, 62-, 75-, or 100-mile route.

▪▪▪▪ DON'T FORGET

Michigan is on eastern time, one hour ahead of Chicago.

When driving around New Buffalo and Three Oaks, tune in to **Radio Harbor Country at 106.7 FM**. It's an eclectic, community-run station with programs by everyone from the local nurse to students from Three Oaks Elementary School; lots of blues, jazz, and world beats, too. Because it's low-watt, it can be difficult to access and staticky.

▪▪▪▪ RESOURCES

Harbor Country Chamber of Commerce (269-469-5409; www .harborcountry.org). The Visitors Guide is packed with useful maps, bike routes, and other info. The Web site helps visitors find lodging and has a "hot deals" coupon section for local shops, restaurants, and lodgings.

9 • TOP OF THE DUNES

After you slog up the hulking sand dune, look out over its golden expanse, and have a *Lawrence of Arabia* moment, it's easy to forget you're just a few miles outside Chicago city limits. Then you look into the distance and see a smoke-belching factory, and it all comes crashing back.

That's the dichotomy of Indiana Dunes, a joint state and national park whose 21 miles of Lake Michigan beachfront hold rustling grasses, half-buried cottonwoods, bird-filled marshes, and pine forests. It shocks and awes that this much nature coexists next to Northwest Indiana's bleak, smokestacked landscape of steel mills and oil refineries.

It has always been a struggle to keep industry from encroaching on the Dunes' rare ecosystem. Activists like schoolteacher Dorothy Buell and Illinois senator Paul Douglas fought hard to preserve the area, and in 1966 Congress rewarded their efforts when it designated the Dunes as parkland. They've done a good job—for the most part, visitors can burrow into the parks and forget about the stinky factories surrounding the place.

In summer, sunny beaches are the Dunes' claim to fame, but the area offers much more than just splashing around. Peat-filled bogs and a heron rookery are among the prizes on the hiking trails. Bike paths crisscross the region, and visitors can pedal back roads with the Crank Club. When snow falls, cross-country skiers and snowshoers take over the trails.

It's simple to visit the Dunes as a day trip and still feel like you've had a real getaway. Those who want to make a night of it can camp or pull up the covers at a farmhouse or English manor B&B. And whether you come for the afternoon or the whole weekend, pencil in a side-trip to see the Dark Lord's makers.

▮▮▮▮ GETTING THERE

Indiana Dunes is about 45 miles southeast of Chicago. Take I-90/94 east from downtown. Follow I-90 east when it splits off (around 63rd Street) toward Indiana. Stay on I-90 for roughly 30 miles, and be prepared to pay tolls en route. Take exit 21 to merge onto I-94 east (toward Detroit). Soon after take exit 22B to merge onto US 20 east toward Porter. This will get you to the middle of the park near the visitor center.

An alternate route is to take Lake Shore Drive south, following the US 41 signs through the South Side. Right after the Indiana border US 41 connects with US 12/US 20 and heads straight to the Dunes. The trip takes about an hour.

Public transportation is an option if you don't mind walking a mile or more from the various stations to the beaches. **Metra South Shore Line trains** (800-356-2079; www.nictd.com) depart frequently from Millennium Station in the Loop and stop at Miller, Portage/Ogden Dunes, Dune Park, and Beverly Shores. Fares cost $5.50–7.50 one way.

▌▌▌▌ GETTING AROUND

The Dunes stretch from Gary in the east to Michigan City in the west. US 12 connects them and is also the road by which you can reach most sites in the area. As you travel on nearby highways, watch for brown signs that direct you to the parks' attractions.

Parking at the national lakeshore's beach lots is difficult on weekends unless you arrive before 10 AM. The exception is West Beach, which has 600 parking spots compared to other beaches' combined 400 spots. West Beach, however, is the only one to charge a fee ($6 per car in summer, free the rest of the year).

▌▌▌▌ NORTHERN INDIANA'S B.O.

Ever wonder what that not-so-pleasant odor is when you drive on the highway through Gary, the one that smells like a giant, perpetually lingering fart? It's sulfur from the area's factory emissions, and it's the same element that makes rotten eggs and, yes, farts stink. It wafts from northern Indiana's pungent combination of industries: the BP oil refinery in Whiting; the U.S. Steel Plant in Gary, churning out some 8 million tons of steel per year; and local chemical and agricultural product plants. Together they form a heady, roll-up-your-window brew.

The smell likely won't go away any time soon. There is no rule—state or federal, not even the Clean Air Act—that addresses odor.

■■■■ WHERE TO STAY

Tryon Guesthouse (219-879-3618
www.tryonfarmguesthouse.com),
1400 Tryon Road, Michigan City
(off IN 212 between US 12 and I-
94). A pastoral landscape of
prairies, woods, meadows, and
ponds surrounds this turn-of-
the-century redbrick farmhouse.
The B&B has five simple bedrooms, each with a private bathroom and wireless access. Breakfast is big enough to feed the
hungriest farmhand, with eggs
from the farm's chicken coop. The
guesthouse is part of a larger
conservation community in
which 50 families share farm
duties and an organic garden.
Rooms including breakfast cost
$68–178.

 Gray Goose Inn (219-926-5781,
800-521-5127; www.graygooseinn
.com), 350 Indian Boundary
Road, Chesterton. This flowery,
eight-room B&B fills an old English country manor on a small
lake. All rooms have queen beds,
private bathrooms, and wireless
access. The suites add a fireplace
and Jacuzzi to the mix. The Goose
is child- and pet-friendly, and
staff will pick you up at the train
station with advance notice. It's
located about 2.5 miles from the
Dunes. Rooms and suites including breakfast cost $110–185 on
weekdays, $115–195 on weekends.

■■■■ CAMPING

**Indiana Dunes State Park
Campground** (219-926-1952;
www.dnr.in.gov/parklake), IL 49,
near Chesterton. Open year-
round. The 140 campsites sit close
together, and though they're in
the woods they don't feel particularly remote. The bright side:
it's only a half-mile walk to the
beach. All sites have electricity
and share two modern bath-
room/shower buildings. The
camp store with groceries is open
Apr. through Oct.; firewood is
available year-round. If you're
coming by train, the grounds are
about 2 miles from the Dune Park
station. Be sure to reserve ahead
(866-622-6746; www.indiana
.reserveworld.com) in summer.
Visitors arriving by car must have
a vehicle permit, which costs $10/
day or $46/year. Campsites cost
$17 Sun. through Wed., $25 Thurs.
through Sat., $28 on holidays.

 Dunewood Campground (219-
926-7561, 800-959-9174; www
.nps.gov/indu), US 12 and Broadway Avenue, near Beverly Shores.
Open Apr. 1 through Oct. 31. This
is the national lakeshore's campground. It's quieter and woodsier
than the state park facility (see
above), but it's also farther from
the beach (about 1.5 miles). The
grounds have 54 drive-in and 25
walk-in sites. There's no electrici-

ty, but there are modern showers and restrooms. A gas station and convenience store are nearby. Sites are first-come, first-served and cost $15.

▪▪▪▪ EATING OUT

It's tough to find a quality meal in the area, though there are a few exceptions.

Lucrezia (219-926-5829), 428 South Calumet Road, Chesterton. Open Sun. through Thurs. 11 AM–10 PM, Fri. and Sat. 11 AM–11 PM. People love this lively trattoria dishing up Northern Italian favorites. Pastas come tossed with veal meatballs, scallops, or porcini mushrooms, among others. Entrées are staples like chicken Vesuvio and veal marsala. Wine and martinis accompany the dishes, along with a full array of Italian desserts and coffees. The outdoor dining area is the place to be when the weather warms. Pastas, $12–15; mains, $17–27; desserts, $5–7.

Miller Bakery Cafe (219-938-2229), 555 South Lake Street, Miller Beach. Open for lunch Tues. through Fri. 11:30 AM–2 PM, dinner Tues. through Thurs. 5 PM–9 PM, Fri. and Sat. 5 PM–10 PM, Sun. 4 PM–8 PM. Locals simply call it "The Bakery," which doesn't come close to describing the sophisticated fare. Small plates include

items like "wood-grilled organic quail stuffed with apple and prosciutto and served on lentils with a cherry liqueur-green peppercorn demi-glace." Entrées include seasonal game and spice-rubbed, truffle-glazed lamb shank. Martinis and wine flow abundantly. Despite the highbrow food, the café has a warm, casual ambience. Small plates, $7–10; lunch mains, $11–16; dinner mains, $18–29.

Shoreline Brewery (219-879-4677), 208 Wabash Street, Michigan City. Open Sun. through Thurs. 11 AM–11 PM, Fri. and Sat. 11 AM–2 AM. This place won't knock

Rustling grasses and half-buried cottonwood trees set the lakefront scene.
PHOTOGRAPH BY LISA BERAN

your socks off, but let's face it—if you're not up to driving to Three Floyd's (see Nearby, page 81) you'll have to make do here. You can get a sampler of three different beers in small glasses. The menu consists of wraps, pastas, fish and chips, meaty entrées, and a fair number of vegetarian dishes like eggplant steak. Burgers and sandwiches, $8–10; mains, $12–22.

Three Floyd's Brewery boils up wild beers.

Kids and gulls alike appreciate a good wave.

PHOTOGRAPH BY LISA BERAN.

▮▮▮▮ WHAT TO SEE AND DO

Parks: Two parks comprise the Dunes—one national, and one state-run. The larger is **Indiana Dunes National Lakeshore** (800-959-9174; www.nps.gov/indu), with 15,000 acres of beaches, dunes, woods, and wetlands that are major habitats for birds and an insane variety of plant life. Everything from cactus to arctic berries to hardwood forests sprouts here. **Indiana Dunes State Park** (219-926-1952; www .dnr.in.gov/parklake) is a 2,100-acre shoreside pocket within the national lakeshore. It has more amenities but is also more regulated and crowded. Both parks are open year-round. Admission to the national park is free, except for West Beach, which charges $6 per car in summer. Admission to the state park costs $10 per car, or $2 per person on foot or bike. An annual pass costs $46 per car.

Beaches: The national lakeshore has eight developed beaches, and on summer weekends they draw big crowds. **Mt. Baldy Beach** is the busiest of the lot. That's because it boasts the highest dunes, with shifting namesake Mt. Baldy offering the best views all the way to Chicago from its 120-foot peak. It's a must to climb, though it will punish your leg muscles. **Central Beach** is only 1 mile away from Mt. Baldy, but it's surprisingly quiet and free of the masses; it's backed by steep dune cliffs. And just so you know: that tower spewing smoke? It's not nuclear, but rather Michigan City's coal-powered electric plant and cooling tower. **Lake View Beach** has a nice terrace and picnic tables. **Kemil Beach** is where the 20-something crowd hangs out. **West Beach**—the farthest west—is the only national lakeshore beach with lifeguards and an admission fee ($6/1 per car/pedestrian in summer, free the rest of the year), plus hiking trails. All of the beaches have bathrooms, but beyond that, facilities are limited and parking can be tough (see Getting Around, page 75, for details).

The national lakeshore surrounds a couple of Gary city beaches that have fine stretches of sand. **Miller Beach** and **Lake Street Beach** are side by side in Marquette Park, which has snacks, decent parking, historic sites, lagoons, and a boat launch.

The **Dunes State Park beach** takes up the final slice of shore. It offers a full set of amenities— lifeguards, showers, a snack bar, picnic tables, and parking lot— but you must pay the park admission ($10 per car, $2 per pedestrian) to get in.

No matter where you are on the lakefront, be careful of rip currents. And no matter what beach you're on, listen for the low hum of the "singing sands," an unusual sound caused by the zillions of sand grains hitting each other in the wind.

Hiking: The national lakeshore has several miles of trails. The 5-mile walk at **Cowles Bog Trail** is the lakeshore's most rugged (though it's still fairly moderate), trekking through marshes and dunes before arriving at an isolated beach. The easy, 2-mile **Heron Rookery Trail** saunters past a breeding ground for the great blue heron; it's located inland, east of Buell Visitor Center. The tall, noble birds can be shy and hard to find, so it's wise to stop into the Buell center first and have staff give you sighting tips. Wildflowers carpet the rookery grounds in spring.

The 2.5-mile **Bailly/Chellberg Trail** winds through the forest not far from the visitor center, passing a restored fur-trading outpost from the 1820s and a farm built by Swedes in the 1870s.

West Beach offers multiple paths, including the bird-rich, 1.6-mile **Long Lake Trail**, which circles around an inland lake. Some of the beach's other trails go through the forest. On damp days the woods smell lovely, and the pines rustling in the breeze are soothing balm for city ears plagued with noise.

The hike to damp, mossy **Pinhook Bog** must be done with park rangers on a guided walk. Contact the Buell Visitor Center for the schedule.

Not to be outdone, the state park offers seven numbered trails that zigzag over 16 miles. Trail 4 (.75 miles) scales Mt. Tom, the highest dune at 192 feet. Trail 2 (3 miles) veers inland and is known for spring flowers, ferns, and cross-country skiing. Steep, breath-sapping Trail 8 (1.75 miles) climbs three of the highest dunes and rewards with fine views of the region. Pick up trail maps at the Buell center (see Resources, page 82).

Biking: The 9-mile, crushed-gravel **Calumet Bike Trail** runs west from near Michigan City almost to the Chellberg Farm in the Dunes' midst. It and other routes are outlined in the free, useful **Northwest Indiana Bike Map** (219-763-6060; www.nirpc .org/transportation/nonmotorized .htm). Unfortunately, the parks do not rent bicycles. The closest option is **Chesterton Bicycle Station** (219-926-1112), 116 South 4th Street, Chesterton, where rentals cost $15 per day. The **Calumet Crank Club** (www.bicycling.org)

hosts free guided rides on weekends ranging from 25 to 75 miles; they pedal into the parks and between the region's towns. The club posts its schedule online. Note the traffic and narrow shoulders on US 12 can make cycling on that road dangerous.

Winter activities: Cross-country skiers glide over the Calumet Trail (see Biking, above). The state park grooms its trails for skiers and snowshoers. Devil's Slide in the state park is the only hill on which sledding is permitted. Visitors must bring all of their own winter equipment, as no rentals are available.

Outlet shopping: **Lighthouse Place Premium Outlets** (219-879-6506; www.premiumoutlets.com /lighthouseplace), 601 Wabash Street, Michigan City. Open Mon. through Sat. 9 AM–9 PM, Sun. 10 AM–6 PM. More than 120 outlet stores stock this mall's faux village buildings, including Adidas, Burberry, Coach, Gap, Puma, J. Crew, Nike, and South Bend Chocolate Company. It's the typical outlet scene—decent prices if you don't mind older styles, and hit or miss whether you find anything to your liking. It might be worth downloading a map ahead of time to plot your attack, since it can be confusing to find certain stores once you're on-site.

▮▮▮▮ HISTORIC SITES

Bailly Homestead and Chellberg Farm (219-926-7561), Mineral Springs Road (between US 12 and US 20). The 1822 log homestead belonged to French Canadian voyageur and fur trader Joseph Bailly. Fifty years later, Swedish immigrants Anders and Johanna Chellberg started a farm nearby. The Bailly-Chellberg Trail connects the two sites. The farm hosts family-friendly activities on weekends. For example, visitors can help feed the pigs and horses Fri. through Sun. from 4 PM–5 PM Mar. through Oct. Call for other scheduled events.

▮▮▮▮ DON'T FORGET

Indiana Dunes is on central time—the same as Chicago—though most of Indiana is on eastern time.

▮▮▮▮ SPECIAL EVENTS

Mid-March: Maple Sugar Festival (www.nps.gov/indu). Demonstrations on how to tap trees and release the sweet stuff at Chellberg Farm.

Early September: Calumet Crank Club Lakeshore Century (www.bicycling.org). Join the group's 25- to 100-mile bike rides along the shore followed by a chili feast.

Mid-September: Duneland Harvest Festival (www.nps.gov/indu). Turn-of-the-century farm activities, crafts, and music at Chellberg Farm.

▮▮▮▮ NEARBY

Three Floyd's Brewpub (219-922-4425; www.threefloydspub.com), 9570 Indiana Parkway, Munster, about 25 miles west of the Dunes. Open Tues. through Fri. 11:30 AM–12 AM, Sat. 12 PM–12 AM, Sun. 12 PM–10 PM. Three Floyd's boils up bold beverages. Its fans are so die-hard they line up by the hundreds on the one day per year the brewery releases its Dark Lord Stout (known as Dark Lord Day, in late April and accompanied by a festival). You never know what'll be on tap, but likely candidates are Alpha King Pale Ale and Robert the Bruce Scottish Ale. The food menu lets you soak it up with creative sandwiches, cones of saucy fries, brick-oven-fired pizzas, and seasonally changing chicken and seafood dishes—many of which incorporate house brews into their recipes. Brewery tours take place on Sat. at 3 PM for $1 and include a free sample. Note you cannot buy carry-out beers on Sun. (Hoosier state law). Pints, $4–5; burgers and sandwiches, $7.50–9; pizzas, $12–16; mains, $16–18.

To reach Three Floyd's from the Dunes, take I-80/94 west toward

Chicago, and get off at Calumet Avenue South. Follow it for 2.5 miles to Superior Avenue and turn right (west). Go two blocks to Indiana Parkway, and turn left. Three Floyd's is under the water tower.

■■■■ RESOURCES

Dorothy Buell Visitor Center (219-926-7561, 800-959-9174), IN 49 (near its intersection with US 20). Open daily 8:30 AM—6 PM in summer, 8:30 AM—4:30 PM the rest of the year. This facility in the national lakeshore has free maps and guides on beaches, hiking, biking, birding, and ecotourism.

The center also has the schedule of ranger-guided walks and Chellberg Farm activities, as well as day programs taking place at the Paul H. Douglas Center for Environmental Education.

Porter County Convention and Visitors Bureau (800-283-8687; www.indianadunes.com). To receive the maps, hiking, and other guides available in the Buell Visitor Center—as well as lodging info and attractions coupons—*before* your arrival, contact the CVB and they'll send them to you gratis.

10 • OARS, POURS, AND MORE IN DOOR COUNTY

Don't let the white picket fences, tidy clapboard houses, small cow-dotted farms, and cherry tree orchards fool you. Door County looks Norman Rockwell quaint, but underneath beats the heart of an adventure sport hot spot. Five state parks with bluff-side hiking trails, off-road bike trails, sea cave kayaking, and backcountry camping cater to outdoor softies and hard-core sportsfolk alike. Outfitters stand ready to help with equipment rentals year-round. Afterward, fine food and drink await to help you celebrate the day's deeds.

Door County has always been an adventure. In the days of yore, just reaching its shores required prodigious feats of navigation through treacherous, wind-bashed waters. The straits around the county's northern edge were so perilous and claimed so many lives the Native Americans called it Death's Door—the latter part of which became the county's name.

The county spreads across a narrow peninsula jutting 75 miles into Lake Michigan. **Sturgeon Bay** lies at the base and is the area's largest town and adminis-trative hub. Shipbuilding is big business here, especially yachts, and it's not uncommon for royal family members from countries like Spain to jet in and check up on their $38 million boats. For vacationers, though, it's the least exciting place to stay on the peninsula.

The real action starts beyond Sturgeon Bay, when the road splits and visitors take their pick of Door County's two sides: the bay side (as in the waters of Green Bay lapping the shore) or lake side (where Lake Michigan does the lapping). The bay side has the busier, cutesy, fudge-shop persona. It's also about 10 degrees warmer. The lake side has less action and more scenery. It's known as the "quiet side." Sunsets happen over the bay, sunrises over the lake, and they're both pretty dang lovely.

Door County's distinct towns stack up as follows (starting on the bay side, from the south): **Egg Harbor** is the crowd-pleaser thanks to its compact, walkable core bunched with shops and restaurants. Bustling **Fish Creek** launched Door County's tourism force years ago, and it holds the greatest concentration of businesses, plus activity mecca Peninsula State Park. Pretty **Ephraim** sits high on the bluffs overlooking Eagle Harbor; alas, the town serves no alcohol (a legacy from its Moravian founders). On the other hand, fun-loving **Sister Bay** rolls out the welcome mat with rowdy bars, upscale restaurants, and a marina. **Gills Rock** is a noncommercialized village at the end of the peninsula, where fifth-generation Scandinavian families still fish from the docks.

From here, ferries sail the wild waters to **Washington Island**, a 700-person community with beaches, small resorts, and roads for relaxed cycling. More remote is teeny **Rock Island**, a state park with no roads—or cars or bikes or facilities—at all. It's a true getaway for hiking and starry camping.

Back on land, two towns lure visitors on the lake side. **Baileys Harbor** sits to the north and is a bit larger than **Jacksonport**, home to the brave folks who host the annual Polar Bear Plunge.

The communities exercise decent restraint in development. Condos show up in patches, but they don't overwhelm the scene,

and Door County seems to have its head on straight about keeping it that way. Most businesses remain family owned.

Boom times are July, August, and weekends in early October for leaf peeping. About half of all businesses shut down between November and April. The ones that stay open get a winter crowd of snowmobilers and cross-country skiers.

Let's be honest: Door County is a long haul for a getaway. It's worth it, though, with its slew of outdoor activities and state parks, welcoming inns and lodges, creative galleries and theaters, and off-the-beaten-path islands. The supremely useful visitor bureau makes it easy to put it all together. Why not stay for a spell?

▮▮▮▮ GETTING THERE

Door County is 245 miles north of Chicago. Take I-90/94 west from downtown, and follow I-94 west (toward Wisconsin) when it splits off. Stay on the interstate for about 85 miles (paying $2.50 in tolls en route). Just south of Milwaukee I-94 merges with I-43, and you'll follow I-43 north for the next 115 miles to Green Bay. Take exit 185 to merge onto WI 57 north toward Sturgeon Bay, and continue for 43 miles. The trip takes four to four and a half hours to Sturgeon Bay, the county's gateway.

■ ■ ■ ■ GETTING AROUND

Door County has two main highways: WI 57 runs beside Lake Michigan on the peninsula's east side and goes through Jacksonport and Baileys Harbor. WI 42 borders Green Bay's waters on the west side and passes through (from south to north) Egg Harbor, Fish Creek, Ephraim, Sister Bay, and Ellison Bay before heading up to Gills Rock at the peninsula's tip.

It takes one hour to drive the 40 miles from Sturgeon Bay at Door County's south end to Gills Rock at the north end. It takes about 15 minutes to drive between the peninsula's east and west sides.

To reach Washington Island and Rock Island you'll need to hit the water. The **Washington Island Ferry** (920-847-2546, 800-223-2094; www.wisferry.com) departs from Northport Pier near Gills Rock every half hour in summer from 8 AM to 6:45 PM, and on a reduced schedule the rest of the year (via an icebreaker in winter!). Round-trip tickets for the 30-minute crossing cost $11 for adults, $5.50 for children, plus $4 per bike or $24 per car.

The **Rock Island Ferry** (920-535-0122) departs from Jackson Harbor on Washington Island. It's a passenger-only vessel (you can leave your car or bike in the parking lot by the dock), and it departs hourly between 10 AM and 4 PM in summer and on a reduced schedule in May, September, and the first half of October, after which it stops running for the season. Round-trip tickets for the 15-minute crossing cost $9 for adults, $5 for children.

■ ■ ■ ■ WHERE TO STAY

The visitor bureau Web site (www .doorcounty.com) provides contact info and descriptions of properties including B&Bs, inns, hotels, resorts, cottages, and private homes. The Web site can also tell you which ones have availability.

Prices listed below are for July and August, the most expensive months. An 11 percent tax is added to all lodging costs. Many properties have a two-night minimum stay requirement. Unless stated otherwise, the places below close for the season between November and April.

Egg Harbor Lodge (920-868-3115, 920-868-3215; www.egg harborlodge.com), 7965 WI 42, Egg Harbor. All rooms have a great water view and patio or balcony from which to appreciate it. Sweet perks include free bike use, a tennis court, putting green, pool, and wireless Internet access. It's a short walk into town for food and drink. Kids and pets are not allowed. Rooms cost $155—195.

Gordon Lodge (920-839-2331, 800-830-6235; www.gordon lodge.com), 1420 Pine Drive, on North Bay (just north of Baileys Harbor). This 130-acre resort has seen some love over the past few years, with upgrades ongoing. It's one of the few places that will let you stay just one night. The lodge itself has 20 retro-themed rooms, some decked out in leopard print. Several rustic wood cottages also dot the premises. The bayside units are for adults only, while the lakeside units are for couples or families and can fit up to six people. All rates include breakfast and complimentary use of the lodge's bikes, kayaks, paddleboats, tennis courts, beach, fishing poles, pool, and hot tub. There's a restaurant/bar on-site, which is handy since the property is isolated. Lodge rooms cost $200, bayside cottages cost $230–260, lakeside cottages cost $150—300.

Eagle Harbor Inn (920-854-2121, 800-324-5427; www.eagle harbor.com), 9914 Water Street, Ephraim. Open year-round. Two types of lodging lie in the inn's white clapboard buildings. A nine-room B&B offers smaller quarters with continental breakfast served in the garden each morning. The inn's suites raise the bar a notch and offer one or two bedrooms furnished with cherrywood beds, a whirlpool, fireplace, kitchen, and private deck; rates for suites do not include breakfast. Children are welcome. B&B rooms cost $98—149; suites with one bedroom cost $199, two bedrooms cost $245.

Beachfront Inn (866-251-0750; www.beachfrontinn.net), WI 57, Baileys Harbor. Open year-round. The Beachfront is a simple motel but earns extra points for its nightly beach bonfires with s'more roasting, and its indoor pool. It's within stumbling distance of several restaurants and bars. Lakefront rooms cost $119—165, side-view rooms cost $84—119, pet-friendly rooms across the street cost $77—95.

Julie's Park Cafe and Motel (920-868-2999; www.juliesmotel .com), 4020 WI 42, Fish Creek. Nothing fancy in the 13 rooms here, but the motel is well located right next to Peninsula State Park and is low-cost for Door County. It allows pets ($15 extra) and has an attached café with wireless Internet access. Rooms cost $79—120.

▪▪▪▪ CAMPING

All of Door County's state parks except Whitefish Dunes have camping. All accept reservations (888-947-2757; www.reserve america.com) for a $10 fee. Entry into the parks by car requires a vehicle permit, which costs $10/day or $35/year.

Peninsula State Park (920-868-3258), by Fish Creek. Open year-round. Peninsula has far and away the most campsites and most amenities. All of the 469 sites are drive-in; 100 of the sites have electrical hookups. There are flush toilets, hot showers, and a camp store. Campsites cost $17, plus $5 for electricity.

Rock Island State Park (920-847-2235), offshore from Washington Island. Open May through mid-Oct. This was voted Wisconsin's best park for walk-in camping. The majority of the island's 40 primitive sites cluster near the ferry dock, but a handful of sites are a mile away across the island. There are no showers, but campers do have access to pit toilets, drinking water, and firewood. Check in at the station on the ferry dock upon arrival. Campsites cost $12–15.

Newport State Park (920-854-2500), by Ellison Bay. Open year-round. Newport has just 16 campsites, but they're all winners scattered along the waterfront.

They're accessible only by backpacking in. Amenities are primitive—no showers, but there are pit toilets and drinking water. Campsites cost $20.

Potawatomi State Park (920-746-2890), by Sturgeon Bay. Open year-round. Potawatomi has 123 drive-in sites (40 with electricity). There are hot showers and flush toilets. Campsites cost $17, plus $5 for electricity.

▪▪▪▪ EATING OUT

You probably keep hearing about the "fish boil," a Door County tradition started by Scandinavian lumberjacks, in which whitefish, potatoes, and onions are cooked in a cauldron over an open flame outdoors. Not much happens until the chef pours kerosene on the flames, and then whoosh! A giant fireball shoots up and creates the "boilover" (which gets rid of the fish oil), and with that, dinner is ready. Several restaurants host dinnertime fish boils, and they're all similar in terms of the experience, food quality, and cost (around $16 per person, all you can eat).

Cherry pie is another Door specialty, at its prime during the mid-July through mid-August cherry-picking season.

Village Cafe (920-868-3342), 7918 WI 42, Egg Harbor. Open daily 7 AM–8 PM in summer, 8 AM–

2 PM the rest of the year. The café's massive menu includes kid-sized meals, vegan burgers, traditional pot roasts, turkey Reubens, chicken potpies, and even a vegetarian offshoot of butternut squash potpie. Breakfast is the house specialty, and the omelets, thick-cut French toast, and homemade granola are served all day. Beer and wine are available. Breakfast, $6–9; burgers and sandwiches, $6.50–8.50; dinner mains, $14–16.

Wilson's Restaurant and Ice Cream Parlor (920-854-2041), 9990 Water Street, Ephraim. Open daily II AM–9 PM mid-May through late Oct., closed the rest of the year. Look for the red-and-white striped awning, which heralds this old-fashioned eatery known for its made-on-the-premises root beer, fried cheese curds, and burgers. Each of the antique booths has its own jukebox that plays 45s. By all means save room for the ice cream, which comes in the form of sundaes, milk shakes, floats, or good ol' scoops in a parfait glass (perfect for flavors like Peanut Butter Explosion). Burgers and sandwiches, $6–8.75; sundaes, $4.25–5.25.

Shoreline Restaurant (920-854-2950), WI 42, Gills Rock. Open daily II AM–9 PM late Apr. through mid-Nov., closed the rest of the year. Shoreline's big bay windows provide gorgeous water views (especially at sunset), and the knotty pine interior is homey as can be. The extensive menu includes fish, chicken, and grilled meat plates, burgers and sandwiches, and a fair number of vegetarian options like Thai curry stir-fry. The luscious cherry pie comes from Sweetie Pies (see below). Burgers and sandwiches, $6–10; dinner mains, $13–19.

Inn at Kristofer's (920-854-9419), 734 Bay Shore Drive, Sister Bay. Open 5 PM–9 PM year-round, closed Tues. Chef Terri Milligan might well visit your table and tell you firsthand about how the morel mushrooms floating in your soup were picked that morning, or how the cashew-encrusted whitefish on your plate was hauled in at Gills Rock a few hours earlier. For dessert, pray it's the season for her cherry-blackberry pie sided by homemade cherry-chip ice cream. Kristofer's is exquisite, upscale dining, but the vibe remains friendly and low-key. Chef Terri also offers cooking classes on-site, both demonstration ($38) and participatory ($138). Mains, $21–31; desserts, $7.95.

Sweetie Pies (920-868-2743, 877-868-2744), 9106 WI 42, Fish Creek. Open daily 9 AM–5 PM in summer, weekends only the rest of the year. In a land way too prone to gloppy, gelatinous cherry pie, Sweetie does Door County proud with its thin, flaky crust and tart natural fillings. The shop usually has several fruity flavors in stock. You can also learn to bake your own though winter pie-baking classes; call for the schedule. Pies, $19.

■■■■ DRINKING

Door County has a couple of locally sourced beverages worth quaffing. For beer, Capital Brewery's "Island Wheat" uses grain grown on Washington Island exclusively for the suds (though it's brewed in Madison). "Death's Door" vodka and gin are also made with Washington Island grains and berries (though they, too, are distilled elsewhere).

JJ's (920-854-4513), 10951 North Bay Shore Drive, Sister Bay. Open daily 11 AM–2 AM in summer, only Wed. through Sat. the rest of the year. Young, boater types hang off the bar stools at this jam-packed, good-time pub. It's famed for a shot called the Bernie ($2), in which one licks a cinnamon-and-sugar-sprinkled orange slice, then slams a tequila shot. When the bell rings, it means someone has bought Bernies for the bar, so prepare your liver. There's a real JJ, too—James Johnson, who has owned the pub (which also serves Mexican food) for more than 30 years.

Bayside Tavern (920-868-3441), WI 42 in downtown Fish Creek. Open daily 11 AM–2 AM in summer, reduced hours the rest of the year. The Bayside is an old-school watering hole, with a long oak bar snaking through the center of the room and locals bellied up for brews and burgers all around it. There's live music and a small cover charge on some nights; the jukebox rules the rest of the time.

Shipwrecked (920-868-2767), 7791 Egg Harbor Road, Egg Harbor. Open daily 11 AM–10 PM in summer, reduced hours the rest of the year. While sipping a

Setting dinner aflame during a fish boil

Mmm, fresh-baked pie made with Door County cherries

house-made Copper Ale, ask the bartender about the ghosts who roam the microbrewery. Or go whole hog and order the six-beer sampler (3 ounces each), served atop a wood plank.

▮▮▮▮ WHAT TO SEE AND DO

Parks: Door County is Wisconsin's richest in state parks, with "five jewels in the crown." The queen bee is massive **Peninsula State Park** (920-868-3258), by Fish Creek, which is loaded with activities year-round. You can bike the Sunset Trail; hike along bluffs on the Eagle Trail (or 20 miles of other paths); swim, sail, and kayak at Nicolet Bay; visit Eagle Bluff Lighthouse; golf the shore-hugging public course; see a show at American Folklore Theatre. And that's just in summertime. In winter you can cross-country ski, snowshoe, sled, tube, snowmobile, and ice fish. All activities are described in more detail in the sections that follow.

Whitefish Dunes State Park (920-823-2400), south of Jacksonport, is a mega-popular day-use area for families thanks to its wide beach fringed with grassy dunes. At the Big Red Tent pavilion, naturalists answer questions about native flora and fauna. Adjacent Cave Point County Park

is a scenic spot to watch the waves smash into the caves beneath the shoreline cliffs.

Remote **Rock Island State Park** (920-847-2235) is quite a trek to get to, requiring two ferry rides off Door County's northern tip (see Getting Around, page 85). The payoff is a rustic, car- and bike-free wooded isle (all of which is parkland) that's wonderful for walking, swimming, camping, and unfettered stargazing.

Secluded **Newport State Park** (920-854-2500) is the second-quietest park after Rock Island, located near Ellison Bay on the peninsula's northern end. It has a beautiful beach, 30 miles of hiking trails (15 miles of which double as off-road bike trails), cross-country ski and snowshoe trails, a nature center, and year-round, walk-in-only camping.

Potawatomi State Park (920-746-2890) is located near Sturgeon Bay on the peninsula's southern end. It offers the full gamut of summer and winter activities, and is well-known for its fishing.

Entry to any of the state parks requires a vehicle permit, which costs $10/day or $35/year.

Lighthouses: Ten lighthouses rise up along Door County's shore. **Cana Island Lighthouse**, on County Road Q near Baileys

Harbor, is the cream of the crop. You can climb to the top of the tall white tower—about 98 stairs—and out onto the walkway where the wind roars and the view drops the jaw. The lighthouse stands out on a causeway, with little paths darting in and around it. It's open daily 10 AM–5 PM early May through late Oct. Admission costs $4.

Eagle Bluff Lighthouse in Peninsula State Park is less dramatic —more houselike than towerlike— but it's easy to reach and offers tours three times per hour. It's open 10 AM–4 PM mid-May through mid-Oct. Admission costs $4.

Folks line up to climb to the top of Cana Island Lighthouse, one of 10 in Door County.
PHOTOGRAPH FROM DOOR COUNTY VISITOR BUREAU

The 1836 **Pottawatomie Lighthouse** on Rock Island is the county's oldest lighthouse, but you'll need the better part of a day to reach it. The journey entails lots of driving, two ferry rides, and a 1.25-mile walk up a hill. Admission is free if you make it that far.

The visitor bureau (see Resources, page 94) has a lighthouse brochure with further information. It's also available by download at www.doorcounty .com/arts-culture/lighthouses .aspx.

Biking: Pedaling through Door County is rewarding, but it's difficult to get away from car traffic. A **Backroad Bike Map** from the visitor bureau (see Resources, page 94) can help; it's available on-site or via download. For dedicated bikeways, the 10-mile **Sunset Trail** in Peninsula Park is a winner, looping by woods, waterfront, and a lighthouse. It has a couple of hills, but for the most part it's nice and easy. And for whatever reason, you don't have to pay the usual state trail fee to ride on it. Rent shiny new hybrid bikes at **Nor Door Sport and Cyclery** (920-868-2275; www .nordoorsports.com), 4007 WI 42, Fish Creek, right across from the Sunset Trail entrance. They cost $6 per hour, $25 per day.

Sailing and kayaking: Kayaking hot spots are at Cave Point

County Park around the sea caves, and at Nicolet Beach, where kayakers launch for the 2-mile paddle to Horseshoe Island. **Bayshore Outdoor Store** (920-854-9220; www.kayakdoorcounty .com), 2457 South Bay Shore Drive, Sister Bay, offers guided tours to both places. The three-hour trips cost $48 per person. The company also rents watercraft from its Nicolet Beach outpost if you want to head out on your own. Sailboats cost $30 per hour, hydro-bikes $18 per hour, and kayaks $12 per hour.

Door County Kayak Tours (920-868-1400; www.doorcounty kayaktours.com), WI 42 in Egg Harbor, is another outfitter—one with a hippyish, eco-conscious slant. Guided tours go to similar destinations and also cost $48 per person; tours that combine yoga with kayaking cost $58 per person.

Shipwreck exploration: More than 200 sunken ships litter the coast around Door County, compliments of the rough waters and perilous currents that thrashed boats before modern navigation devices helped keep the destruction in check. As you drive around the peninsula, keep an eye out for **Maritime Trail** kiosks that mark where the wrecks are located offshore. Two affiliated Web sites—www.maritimetrails .org and www.wisconsinship

wrecks.org—also provide information, including underwater maps of wreck sites for divers, and locations of near-shore wrecks you can swim or kayak to from shore. An example of the latter is at Garrett Bay near Gills Rock, where the 1888 *Fleetwing* rests.

Golfing: You can't throw a tee in Door County without it landing on a golf course. The peninsula has 11 courses; the visitor bureau under the name **Door County Golf** (920-743-4456, 800-527-3529; www.doorcountygolf.com) provides details. Most courses accept walk-ons, though reservations are advised, especially at scenic **Peninsula State Park Golf Course** (920-854-5791), where you play 18 holes right on the waterfront.

Art-making: Artists' studios and galleries make frequent appearances throughout the county, along with ample opportunities to do it yourself. **The Clearing** (877-854-3225; www .theclearing.org), WI 42, Ellison Bay, is a folk school (no grades or credits) that teaches woodworking, painting, photography, jewelry making, and other arts to adults through day classes and weeklong, live-on-site workshops. At **Hands On Art Studio** (920-868-9311, 888-868-9311; www.handsonartstudio.com),

3655 Peninsula Players Road, Fish Creek, you can walk in off the street and create something artsy in just a few hours. Choose from mosaics, pottery, glass, and furniture painting among others; buy the materials on-site, and the instructors help you put it all together. The studio welcomes adults and kids alike. It's especially friendly to the latter, since it's situated on a farm with llamas and other animals.

Theater: Several theater troupes put on a show in Door County. **American Folklore Theater** (920-854-6117; www.folklore theatre.com) in Peninsula State Park is the most fun. The group performs Midwest-themed original musical comedies like *Guys on Ice* (about ice fishermen) and *Lumberjacks in Love* in an open-air facility. Other troupes doing the outdoor thing include **Door Shakespeare** (920-839-1500; www.doorshakespeare.com) near Baileys Harbor, and the **Peninsula Players** (920-868-3287; www .peninsulaplayers.com) near Fish Creek, who stage everything from Neil Simon to Chekhov. The season typically runs from mid-June through late August (though the Peninsula Players go until early October), and tickets cost $16/23/29 for Folklore, Shakespeare, and the Peninsula Players, respectively.

Movie watching: **Skyway Drive-In Theatre** (920-854-9938; www.doorcountydrive-in.com), on WI 42 between Fish Creek and Ephraim, screens a first-run double feature nightly in summer and on weekends in May, September, and through mid-October. Bring lawn chairs and a portable radio (to play the sound), and you'll greatly enhance your viewing pleasure. Tickets cost $6.75 for adults, $3.75 for children.

Winter activities: Door County's parks barely slow down in winter. Bundle up and make tracks by cross-country skiing, snowshoeing, snowmobiling, tubing, and ice fishing. By Peninsula State Park's entrance **Nor Door Sport and Cyclery** (920-868-2275; www.nordoorsports .com), 4007 WI 42, Fish Creek, rents skis, snowshoes, and tubes for $25/15/10 per day, respectively.

▪▪▪▪ SPECIAL EVENTS

Early January: Polar Bear Plunge (www.doorbell.net/pbc), Jacksonport. On January 1 at noon, 800 hardy souls clear away ice chunks and jump in Lake Michigan to ring in the new year (and raise money for charity).

Mid-May: Lighthouse Walk (www .dcmm.org/lhw.html), countywide. Lighthouses normally closed to visitors fling open their doors for this special weekend.

Mid-June: Fyr Ball Festival (www.ephraim-doorcounty.com), Ephraim. Based on an old Scandinavian tradition, the fest celebrates the beginning of summer with the burning of the winter witch and fireworks.

▮▮▮▮ NEARBY

You'll skirt **Green Bay** (920-494-9507, 888-867-3342; www.packer country.com) before turning north for Door County. A trip on into town means paying homage to the Green Bay Packers' Lambeau Field, where some of the most butt-freezing games in NFL history have been played. The **Packer Hall of Fame** (920-569-7512; www.packers.com) has football movies and interactive exhibits. Admission costs $10 for adults, $5 for children.

Train buffs can chug out to the **National Railroad Museum** (920-437-7623; www.nationalrrmuseum .org), 2285 South Broadway Street, which displays massive steam and diesel locomotives, remnants of Green Bay's glory days as a freight-shipping center. Admission includes train rides in summer. The cost is $9 for adults, $6.50 for children.

▮▮▮▮ RESOURCES

Door County Visitor Bureau (920-743-4456, 800-527-3529; www.doorcounty.com), 1015 Green Bay Road, Sturgeon Bay (the entrance is off WI 57/42). Open Mon. through Thurs. 8 AM– 5 PM, Fri. 8 AM–7 PM, Sat. and Sun. 10 AM–4 PM mid-May through mid-October, reduced hours the rest of the year. It's an excellent resource, both in person and online, with loads of special-interest brochures on lighthouses, golf courses, biking routes, art galleries, and much more. The bureau also helps visitors find lodging.

LEARN

11 • FAST BREAK:
Oak Park's Famous Sons

A wealth of culture floats around Oak Park, compliments of its two famous sons: architect Frank Lloyd Wright and author Ernest Hemingway.

It's generous of the town to embrace these fellows, since neither was particularly kind to Oak Park.

Wright lived and worked here from 1889 to 1909—the first 20 years of his career, when he developed the Prairie Style that would become his signature design. You know the look—plain, with long, low lines and lots of earth colors, like the Midwest's landscape. Wright designed a heap of Prairie Style homes in town, but he often dismissed them as just a way to earn a quick buck. He split town after a sordid affair (more details on page 98) and never lived here again.

Hemingway was born in Oak Park and lived here until age 20. He famously called his hometown a "village of wide lawns and narrow minds." Oak Park brushed off the slight and honored him with a museum.

In addition to its Wright and Hemingway shrines, the town distinguishes itself with eclectic eats and hip shops tucked into old Art Deco buildings. And because Oak Park knows how to treat a visitor right, it compacts all of these sights, shops, and restaurants into a walkable core.

▪▪▪▪ GETTING THERE

Oak Park is 10 miles (about 20 minutes) west of downtown Chicago. From the Loop, take I-290 west, exiting north on Harlem Avenue; take Harlem north to Lake Street and turn right. A parking garage is available a few blocks down the road at the northeast corner of Lake and Forest Avenue, adjacent to the visitors center. It's free for the first hour, $1 for two hours, and $5 for four hours Monday through Saturday and free all day Sunday. You can also look for free street parking on Forest Avenue; there's a two-hour limit.

It's easy to get here by public transportation. Take the Green Line to its terminus at the Harlem stop, which is about four blocks from the visitors center.

▮▮▮▮ EATING OUT

Jerusalem Cafe (708-848-7734), 1030 Lake Street. Open daily 11 AM–10 PM. This Middle Eastern fast-food joint helps tired sightseers refuel with warm pita, crisp falafel sandwiches, and beef shawarma. Better yet, the chow is accompanied by fresh juices (orange, carrot, and apple among them), fruit smoothies (strawberry, mango, and banana), and Turkish coffee. Juices and smoothies, $3.50–4; mains, $5–8.

Petersen Ice Cream (708-386-6131), 1100 Chicago Avenue. Open daily 11 AM–10 PM. You're going to pay for your premium ice cream in this old-timey shop, but that's okay because it's the real deal with 18 percent butterfat (to compare: Ben and Jerry's has around 17 percent butterfat, while Breyers has around 15 percent). The 30 flavors range from cappuccino to cinnamon to Oreo. It's located a few blocks from the Wright Home and Studio. Cones, $3.25–4.35.

Hemmingway's Bistro (708-524-0806), 211 North Oak Park Avenue. Open daily 7 AM–10 PM. Located across from the Hemingway Museum in the historic 1920s Write Inn, Hemmingway's (note the extra "m") makes you feel you've wandered in from a Parisian side street. The traditional French fare starts with crusty baguettes and great wine. The oysters win raves (and there's a Monday-night oyster bar for true fans), as does the rabbit in mustard sauce. If nothing else, drop in and sit at the bar for a drink. On Sundays, the Champagne Brunch (from 11 AM–3 PM) is a big production. Lunch mains, $8–17; dinner mains, $18–29; Sun. brunch, $27.

▮▮▮▮ WRIGHT SIGHTS

The best way to see them is on foot. The information below lists several of the homes in walking-

The Balch House, a fine example of Frank Lloyd Wright's Prairie Style.

The Home and Studio where Wright launched his career.

tour order. The trek is roughly 2 miles.

Start at the **Oak Park Visitors Center** (see Resources, page 100) at 158 North Forest Avenue. Ask for the architectural site map (a free, photocopied page), which shows the nearby homes' locations. The mile-long stretch on Forest and Chicago Avenues is particularly notable, with 10 Wright designs huddled here. The homes are privately owned, so all gawking must occur from the sidewalk—which you'll be sharing with throngs of Wright-heads from around the globe.

After you leave the visitors center, walk north on Forest Avenue for a short bit. The first Wright homes you'll see are at street **numbers 210 and 238**, which both show his low, flat style. Next up, across the street from each other, are **numbers 313 and 318**.

Next to 313 is **Number 333**, the Moore House—a particularly noteworthy dwelling. It's Wright's bizarre interpretation of an English manor house that was first built in 1895. In his later years, Wright called the house "repugnant" and said he had only taken the commission for the dough. "I gave in to the fact that I had a family and they had a right to live—and their living was up to me," he says in his autobiography. He claimed he walked out of his way to avoid passing it.

The area's most treasured site— the **Wright Home and Studio** (708-848-1976; www.wrightplus .org)—is at 951 Chicago Avenue (the corner of Forest and Chicago). This was where Wright housed his wife and six children, as well as thought up his famous designs between 1889 and 1909. Wright's mentor and first employer, Louis Sullivan, gave him the loan to build the structure. The two later parted ways when Sullivan found out Wright was accepting private commissions behind his back. Wright's tenure in the home ended when he was 42 and ran off to Europe with a female client named Mamah Cheney, leaving behind his family and architecture practice. He set up shop next at Taliesin in Wisconsin (see chapter 5's Nearby section), where he lived with Cheney until a deranged servant murdered her in 1914.

Learn all about the man and his deeds during the hour-long tours held weekdays at 11 AM, 1 PM, and 3 PM, and weekends every 20 minutes between 11 AM and 3:30 PM. Self-guided audio tours of the neighborhood are also available. Tours cost $12 for adults, $5 for children. Wright-heads should buy the Wright Architectural Guide Map of Oak Park and River Forest ($4.35), which provides background not only for the nearby structures but also for several others beyond. It's available in the well-stocked gift shop.

After you leave the Home and Studio, turn left on Chicago Avenue. Three more Wright homes pop up in quick succession at **numbers 1019, 1027, and 1031**.

Retrace your steps on Chicago and then walk one block east to Kenilworth Avenue. Turn left into the park and walk a short bit past it. The 600 block of Kenilworth is where Oak Park's famous sons meet. **Number 611** is Wright's Balch House, one of the first houses he designed upon his adulterous return from Europe. The blue Queen Anne abode at **number 600** was Hemingway's home during his high school years.

Retrace your steps to Chicago Avenue and keep walking east to North Euclid Avenue. Turn right for more Wright mania at **numbers 321, 317, and 223**.

If you walk one block farther down Euclid to Lake Street and turn right, you'll soon reach the **Unity Temple** (708-383-8873; www.unitytemple-utrf.org), 875 Lake Street. Besides the Home and Studio, the temple is the only other Wright building that devotees can go inside. It's open Mon. through Fri. 10:30 AM—4:30 PM for self-guided tours, and Sat. and Sun. 1 PM—4 PM for guided tours on the hour. On various Saturday evenings from Oct. through Apr., the temple hosts live music from classical to country; check the Web site for the schedule and prices. Tours cost $8 for adults, $6 for children.

▌▌▌▌ HEMINGWAY SIGHTS

"Papa" doesn't get the same fanfare as Wright, but then again, he was always a man of few words. His story is told at the low-key **Ernest Hemingway Museum** (708-848-2222; www.ehfop.org), 200 North Oak Park Avenue. Open Sun. through Fri. 1 PM—5 PM, Sat. 10

The Hemingway Museum gives the low-down on Papa and his family.

AM—5 PM. The exhibits begin with his middle-class Oak Park childhood, and move on to cover writings from his time in Spain and during Wold War II. Admission also includes entry to **Hemingway's birthplace** at 339 North Oak Park Avenue (same hours), where you can see his first room. Ernest was born here in 1899 in the large, rambling home of his maternal grandparents. Docents at both sites give tours and provide Hemingway family stories by the earful. Dual admission costs $8 for adults, $6 for children.

▌▌▌▌ SPECIAL EVENTS

Mid-May: Wright Plus Housewalk (www.wrightplus.org). It's the one day per year when visitors get to peek inside the privately owned Wright homes.

▌▌▌▌ RESOURCES

Oak Park Visitors Center (708-848-1500, 888-625-7275; www.visitoakpark.com), 158 North Forest Avenue. Open daily 10 AM—5 PM. Pick up an architectural site map (a free, photocopied page) of nearby Wright homes. Note the audio tours here are *not* the same as those at the Home and Studio; these tours are more broadly focused on Oak Park versus hardcore Wright info.

Loving Frank by Nancy Horan (Ballantine Books: 2007). Fiction and fact mix in this novel about Wright and his Oak Park lover Mamah Cheney.

12 • INDIANA'S AMISH COUNTRY

If they weren't so humble, Northern Indiana's Amish could teach Americans a thing or two about how to go "green." After all, these folks have been growing their own food, saying no to foreign oil, and living off the grid for centuries.

The Indiana community is the nation's third-largest Amish enclave—after those around Holmes County, Ohio, and Lancaster County, Pennsylvania—and it is indeed a different world. Call it life in the past lane.

Descended from conservative 16th-century Dutch-Swiss religious factions, the Amish believe modern conveniences detract from family life, and so they shun things like electricity, telephones, and motorized vehicles. They farm the land with horse and plow and travel by bicycle or horse-drawn buggy. Often referred to as "the plain people," the Amish consider bright colors to be prideful, which is why they sew their modest clothing in shades of gray or pastels, and why they paint most buildings white. However, degrees of strictness vary, and each community negotiates its own rules (including the Mennonites, who share a similar faith with the Amish, but embrace modern amenities).

A trip here, then, is about poking down country roads and absorbing a quieter way of life. Wood-frame farmhouses and tidy barns speckle the fields. Laundry flaps on clotheslines, and horses clip-clop by on the roads. Power lines are scarce, and you can tell which homes are traditional Amish because no wires attach to the dwellings. Local bakeries and craft shops provide hitching posts in addition to parking spaces.

It's idyllic, but that's not to say tourism hasn't hit the area hard. Attractions like the Shipshewana Flea Market draw crowds that trample through, and several nongenuine businesses have sprung up in the region to cash in on the scene. Your best bet to experience the "real" Amish Country is to pick a back road and head down it. Often you'll see families selling beeswax candles, quilts, and fresh produce on their porch.

Shipshewana (population 550) and Middlebury (population 3,000) are the main Amish areas. The former is mostly Amish, while the latter is an even split of Amish and non-Amish cultures. Middlebury is also the place to eat pie—big fat wide flaky creamy slices of pie. Elkhart (population 52,000) is the region's industrial point of entry, and Goshen (population 32,000) gives the area its art injection.

Almost everything closes on Sunday, the time for church and family.

▪▪▪▪ GETTING THERE

Elkhart, the region's gateway, is 115 miles east of Chicago. Take I-90/94 east from downtown. Follow I-90 east when it splits off (around 63rd Street) toward Indiana. Stay on I-90 (which eventually merges with I-80) the whole way. You'll pay about $8 in tolls en route. The trip takes two hours.

▪▪▪▪ GETTING AROUND

From Elkhart, Middlebury lies 15 miles east via US 20, while Shipshewana lies 7 miles farther east via US 20. Goshen is 9 miles southeast via US 33. Between Middlebury and Shipshewana the buggy traffic picks up, so be mindful while driving—a 5-mph buggy is no match for a 65-mph car.

▪▪▪▪ WHERE TO STAY

B&Bs and country inns are the region's lodging forte. The visitors center Web site (www.amish country.org) provides contact information and descriptions for local properties.

Farmstead Inn (260-768-4595; www.farmsteadinn.com), 370 South Van Buren Street, Shipshewana. The Farmstead is plain-Jane outside and in, but perks include the unbeatable location by the flea market, free wireless access (lobby only), continental breakfast, Ping-Pong tables, and a small indoor pool and whirlpool. The 154 rooms are spic-and-span, and the Amish hospitality is first-class. Rooms including breakfast cost $69–129.

Amish Log Cabins (260-768-7770; www.shipshewanacamp ground.com), at the intersection of IN 5 and IN 120, Shipshewana (3.5 miles north of downtown). Open Apr. 1 through Oct. 31. The grounds offer 13 fully furnished "lodging cabins" that sleep two to four people and come equipped with private bathrooms, TVs, and continental breakfast (Mon. through Sat. only). There are also five "rustic cabins" that sleep four people (in two bunk beds and a double bed). These cabins share a bathhouse, and you must bring your own linens. All cabins are handcrafted from pinewood and have a porch swing. Furnished cabins cost $89–109, rustic cabins cost $49.

Country Victorian B&B (574-825-2568, 800-262-7829; www.countryvictorian.com), 435 South Main Street, Middlebury. This is a quintessential cozy, quilt-and-antique-laden B&B, but with beyond-the-norm hospitality. The owners pamper guests with snacks, cookies, and a bountiful breakfast and provide helpful advice on sightseeing. The five rooms have private bathrooms and wireless Internet access. The location is a convenient quarter mile from Middlebury's town center with its pie, quilt, and Amish hat shops. Rooms cost $79–109.

■■■■ CAMPING

Shipshewana Campground (260-768-4669; www.shipshewanacampground.com), 1105 South Van Buren Street, Shipshewana. Open Apr. 15 through Oct. 15. This group owns two campgrounds. One is north with the Amish Log Cabins (see page 102). The other—a.k.a. the South Park location—is just a half mile from the flea market. South Park is also better suited for tents. The grounds have two modern shower houses, flush toilets, electrical hookups, and wireless access (free for 15 minutes, $4 per day after). Campsites cost $26–36.

■■■■ EATING OUT

Village Inn (574-825-2043), 105 South Main Street, Middlebury. Open Mon. through Fri. 5 AM–8 PM, Sat. 5 AM–2 PM. "How's the pie?" the waitress asked. "Mmm, mmm, mmm," the customer replied. That says it all. Experts agree (see Road Tripping for Pie sidebar, page 104) Village Inn's pies are the best in the land— flaky crust, perfect meringue,

An Amish farm near Shipshewana.
PHOTOGRAPH
BY LISA BERAN

▮▮▮▮ ROAD TRIPPING FOR PIE

Sue Anne Zollinger is founder of the Pie of the Month Club (www.pieofthemonth.org), and she gives the lowdown on where to get good pie in the Midwest.

First, some background: Sue Anne is an artist who studied at the Art Institute of Chicago, and she now works as a biologist conducting research in Scotland. She has always loved pie. She started the club in 1993 as a way to keep in touch with far-flung friends and share her pastry passion.

Pie Club members do not get a pie each month, but rather a cool, arty postcard with a quirky pie recipe to do it yourself. Other perks include the coveted membership card to carry in your wallet, and a club T-shirt. The club Web site has a pie database, where members review pie places around the country, and a Pie Expert, where people submit pie-baking questions. Over the years, the club has grown to 300 rabid members.

What makes a good pie, in your opinion?

Hand-rolled crust is critical. I hate these crust rolling and stamping machines. They even make them for small café owners now, so "homemade" pie can look and taste as pasty and prefab as ones you buy in the grocery store. Regardless of the saved time it may afford, the crust is never as good. Never as flaky. You need that human touch to make a good pie.

What characteristics make Midwest pies special?

Well, the Midwest is a mixed bag. The two biggest things that come to mind are meringue-topped cream pies, and the Amish/Mennonite influence. But the southern parts of the Midwest are quite different than the northern parts.

For example, you won't find a cherry pie on the planet as delicious as you will find in Michigan. But cherries are not so commonly grown in southern Illinois or Indiana. Ohio and Indiana are famous for butterscotch pies. Indiana has a unique pie called Sugar Pie, or Sugar Cream Pie. In Iowa you might find cool fluffy chiffon pies. In Nebraska and Minnesota you'll see sour cream raisin pie, something you'd never see in Indiana or Ohio.

Another difference: in the USA's East and West, you're more likely to get whipped cream on top of your cream pie. But in the heart of the Midwest it's usually a billowy mountain of meringue on top. Delicious and beautiful.

Any favorite pie places in the area?

[Note: We've listed all of Sue Anne's recommendations with addresses on the next page.]

I haven't found a great pie place in Chicago proper. Get out of Chicago a bit and you'll have much more luck.

In Wisconsin, the Elegant Farmer makes apple pies that are baked in paper bags. They're fantastic. OJ's Midtown Restaurant also makes a fantastic pie, as does Upper Krust near Madison.

I normally don't expect much from "Amish" restaurant pie, because usually these are mass-produced for tourists and are far from delicious or homemade. But the Village Inn in northeast Indiana is an amazing pie place. You have to get there early—breakfast-time, even—to get any kind of selection. Both times I've been there, it was late lunchtime and there were only one or two pieces of pie left. I also like Farmhouse Pies by Rosemary in Lafayette. She's great, the pies are great.

In Illinois, I've found great pie down south off I-70 toward St Louis, but I admit I haven't looked in the middle of the state. Blue Springs Cafe is worth driving out of your way for. Really breathtaking pies, they're literally a foot high. And totally made from scratch. Deeeee-lish. The Jubilee in Edwards features about 20 pies made fresh daily. We tried three pies—a blackberry, a crumb-topped apple, and an apricot. All three were fantastic. Unfortunately they were sold out of the gooseberry pie, which we heard was the one to die for.

A pie-fanatic friend says the place to get the best Michigan cherry pie, or any other flavor, is Woodland Farm Market in Shelby.

What's the grossest pie flavor you've ever encountered?

Prune Butterscotch Orange Nut pie. It wasn't the worst pie I've ever had, since it was homemade with a nice flaky crust and all that. But it was by far the worst combination of flavors. It was gross—and that's saying a lot from a gal who has eaten pickle pie, sauerkraut pie, orange Tic Tac pie, and turnip pie.

▌▌▌▌ SUE ANNE'S PICKS

Elegant Farmer (262-363-6770), 1545 Main Street, Highways ES and J, Mukwonago, Wisconsin (north of Lake Geneva).

    OJ's Midtown Restaurant (920-855-6395), 128 West Main Street, Gillett, Wisconsin (north of Green Bay).

    Upper Krust (920-206-9202), 1300 Memorial Drive, Watertown, Wisconsin (near Madison).

    Village Inn, Middlebury, Indiana. See Eating Out, page 103.

    Farmhouse Pies by Rosemary (765-471-7008), 551 Beck Lane, Lafayette, Indiana.

    Blue Springs Cafe (618-654-5788), 3505 George Street, Highland, Illinois (east of St. Louis).

    Jubilee Cafe (309-691-7778), Kickapoo-Edwards I-74 Exit 82, Edwards, Illinois (near Peoria).

    Woodland Farm Market (231-861-5380), 5393 West Shelby Road (1 mile west of US 31), Shelby, Michigan (north of Saugatuck).

creamy fillings, huge slices. Mennonite women come in to bake them daily at 4:30 AM, and yes, lard is the secret ingredient. Arrive before lunch to get the best selection, which includes strawberry, peanut butter, Snickers, and the life-changing banana cream. Oh, and Village Inn also serves omelets; pork tenderloin, chicken salad, and tuna melt sandwiches; and smoked pork chops for dinner. But it's gonna be hard to get past that pie. Pull up a chair at the booths or hunker down at the counter. Mains, $3—7; pie slices, $2.05.

Das Dutchman Essenhaus (800-455-9471), 240 US 20, Middlebury. Open Mon. through Thurs. 6 AM—8 PM, Fri. and Sat. 6 AM—9 PM. Indiana's largest restaurant is a bit of a tourist trap. It's known for its all-you-can-eat, traditional Amish dinner of baked steak, fried ham, and chicken and noodles. The attached bakery crams its shelves with 29 types of pie. They're shadows of the Village Inn's pies (see above), but not bad and they'll do in a bind. The whoopie pie (a snack-size confection with sugar-cream filling sandwiched between two cakey chocolate cookies) stands out. Pie slices, $2.60—2.95; breakfast, $4—7; burgers and sandwiches, $4—7; dinner mains, $9—12; all-you-can-eat dinner, $15—17.

Kelly Jae's Cafe (574-537-1027), 133 South Main Street, Goshen. Open for lunch Tues. through Fri. 11:30 AM—1:30 PM, for dinner Tues. through Sat. 5 PM—9 PM. For folks who tire of the meat-and-potato, family-style Amish dining experience, this café—which a well-known area chef opened in 2008—serves tapas and alcohol.

▮▮▮▮ WHAT TO SEE AND DO

It's worth it to download or pick up a CD version of the **Heritage Trail**, a narrated 90-mile, self-guided driving tour through Amish Country. It's sort of cheesy, but it does provide good background on what you're seeing, and it takes you by most major sites and shops. The visitors center (see Resources, page 109) supplies the free CDs; the download is at www.amishcountry.org /heritage.trail.

Shipshewana Auction and Flea Market (260-768-4129; www .shipshewanafleamarket.com), 345 South Van Buren Street, Shipshewana. This huge complex—the focal point of Shipshewana—hosts several activities. The flea market is open Tues. and Wed. 8 AM—5 PM May through Oct. and is one of the nation's largest outdoor bazaars. More than 1,000 vendors sprawl over 50 acres and sell everything from farm tools to nursing bras to birdbaths; food booths help fuel shoppers' sprees. The venue also holds several auctions: antiques go on the block Wed. at 8 AM, livestock Wed. at 10 AM, and horses Fri. at 9 AM. There's also a year-round antique gallery with 100 dealers on-site, as well as the Farmstead Inn (see page 102). Admission is free.

Menno-Hof Visitors Center (260-768-4117; www.mennohof .org), 510 South Van Buren Street,

An Amish buggy heading down a country road near Shipshewana
PHOTOGRAPH BY LISA BERAN

See noodles, honey, and other local products made before your very eyes at Dutch Country Market.

Shipshewana. Open Mon. through Wed. 10 AM—5 PM, Thurs. and Fri. 10 AM—7 PM, Sat. 10 AM—5 PM, reduced hours Jan. through Mar. The Menno-Hof museum provides thorough background information on Amish and Mennonite faith and lifestyles. There's even a glimpse into a typical Northern Indiana Amish home. The visitors center (see Resources, page 109) has coupons for a few bucks off the entrance fee. Admission costs $6 for adults, $3 for children.

Buggy Lane Tours (574-238-4498, 574-825-5474; www.buggy lanetours.com) behind the Blue Gate Restaurant on Van Buren Street, Shipshewana. The tours are kind of hokey, but where else are you going to ride in a buggy? Tours range from a short, seven-minute jaunt around the block to a two-hour visit to milk cows on a local farm. Cost is $4—18 per person.

Gohn Brothers (574-825-2400), 105 South Main Street. Open Mon. through Fri. 8 AM—4:30 PM, Sat. 8 AM—4 PM. Gohn Brothers is a 100-year-old dry goods store that carries "quality, plain clothing" for the Amish. You'll see rows of pants with buttons instead of zippers, wide black hats, and bolts of pastel fabric as you walk over the creaky wood floors.

Dutch Country Market (574-825-3594), 11401 Country Road 16

(1 mile east of Middlebury). Open Mon. through Fri. 8:30 AM—5:30 PM, Sat. 8:30 AM—4 PM. This family-owned market is an authentic place to pick up locally made products. You can watch them crank out the noodles before your very eyes, as well as see bees in the hive producing what will soon become the shop's honey and soap.

Old Bag Factory (574-534-2502; www.oldbagfactory.com), 1100 Chicago Avenue (two blocks north of US 33), Goshen. Open Mon. through Sat. 9 AM—5 PM. The former factory has been converted to arty shops and galleries selling quilts, pottery, furniture, and antiques. The top floor holds the LVD's Concert Hall (www.lvds .info), an intimate venue for folk and bluegrass performances.

RV/Motor Home Hall of Fame (574-293-2344; www.rvmhhallof fame.org), 21565 Executive Parkway (off I-80/90 at exit 96). Open Mon. through Sat. 9 AM—5 PM. Elkhart bills itself as the RV Capital of the World, since more than 100 RV manufacturers are based within a 100-mile radius. This glassy, mondo museum tells the story of how it came to be, showcasing lots of classic and modern RVs in the process. Admission costs $8 for adults, $3 for children.

Marshland Trail Riding (574-536-0651; www.marshlandtrail

riding.com), 17420 US 20, Goshen. Saddle up for one-hour guided horseback rides. The cost is $25 per person.

▋▋▋▋ DON'T FORGET

Amish Country is on eastern time, one hour ahead of Chicago. Also, religious beliefs prohibit the Amish from posing for photographs, so be respectful when snapping pictures in the region.

▋▋▋▋ SPECIAL EVENTS

Late June: Elkhart Jazz Festival (www.elkhartjazzfestival.com). Ragtime, swing, big band, and straight-ahead jazz waft from stages during this three-day event downtown.

Mid-September: Middlebury Fall Festival (www.middleburyin .com). It's a weekend of farmers' markets, crafts, antiques, food, and RV displays.

Late September: Michiana Mennonite Relief Sale (www .mennonitesale.org), Goshen. Hundreds of quilts and woodcrafts go on the auction block to benefit worldwide relief efforts.

▋▋▋▋ RESOURCES

Amish Country/Elkhart County Visitors Center (800-517-9739; www.amishcountry.org), 219 Caravan Road (just north of I-80/90 at exit 92). Open Mon. through Fri. 8 AM–5 PM, Sat. 9 AM–4 PM. Call for a copy of the excellent Vacation Planner, trawl the Web site for lodging and activity information, or stop in to pick up the free driving tour CD, maps, and attraction coupons. Bike rentals are available, too.

13 • ROLLING DOWN ROUTE 66

Buckle in for a trail of corn dogs, giant spacemen, and chatty gas station attendants. Route 66 was the nation's original road trip, and it's still an exceptional ride, rolling through miles of nostalgic and oddball sights.

As America's first paved, cross-country highway, it earned the nicknames "the Mother Road" and "Main Street USA." Its heyday was the 1950s, when most Americans were just starting to own cars. Route 66 took a diagonal path to Los Angeles through the rural landscape of the Midwest and southwest. Pie-filled diners and mom-and-pop motels cropped up to serve the new motorists, offering them a slice of downhome hospitality.

Today, Route 66 time-capsules that small-town America from a half century ago. The road starts amid downtown Chicago's mod skyscrapers, but within a few miles of the big city you start to see it. Granted, it's not easy—Route 66 is almost totally superseded by I-55 in Illinois, and you have to work hard to stay on the byway versus the big, bad interstate. But the old road still exists

in scattered sections, and preservationists are working hard to ensure it stays that way.

We've structured this chapter differently than the book's other chapters, making it a town-by-town road trip. It's divided into roughly 50-mile chunks between Chicago and Springfield—a span filled with first-rate Route 66 kitsch—and all of the places to eat and sightsee are included in the running text rather than broken out into separate sections (as elsewhere in the book). The attractions listed give a taste of the Mother Road, but by no means is this list all-inclusive. Route 66 holds much more, and true road buffs can use the Resources (see page 116) to plan a comprehensive trek—even one that goes all the way to Los Angeles.

Summer is prime time on the road, though most sights are open year-round. You'll likely meet many foreigners making the journey, especially those from England, Germany, and the Netherlands hoping to catch a glimpse of the "real" America. Most are serious road trippers in it for the whole seven-state, 2,400-mile odyssey to Santa Monica Pier at the Pacific Ocean's edge.

▮▮▮▮ CHICAGO TO JOLIET (45 MILES)

The Mother Road starts in downtown Chicago on Adams Street, just west of Michigan Avenue. Look for the **Begin Route 66** sign on Adams's north side as you head west toward Wabash Avenue.

If you're going to do it right, you have to stop a few blocks down the road for breakfast at **Lou Mitchell's** (312-939-3111), 565 West Jackson Boulevard. Open Mon. through Sat. 5:30 AM–3 PM, Sun. 7 AM–3 PM. Lou's serves typical fare—omelets, flapjacks, coffee —but the waitresses who sling it have been around since Route 66 was first paved. The line to get a table can be lengthy, so staff give out free Milk Duds and doughnut holes to ease the wait.

Sugar-fueled and back at the wheel, you'll stay on Adams Street beyond Greektown until you come to Ogden Avenue. Go left, and continue through the 'burbs of Cicero and Berwyn.

Throughout this heavy-traffic area around Chicago, keep an eye on the roadside for the brown "Historic Route 66" signs. They're few and far between, but they do

tend to appear at crucial junctions during the next 30 miles or so.

At Harlem Road, turn left (south) and stay on it briefly until you come to Joliet Road. It runs southwest through suburban commercial corridors. By the time you reach Countryside, you finally start seeing businesses advertise their 66-ness, i.e., the James

This way to fresh-tapped maple sirup (not syrup) in Funk's Grove.

Paul Bunyan and his giant hot dog watch over the small town of Atlanta.

Dean Muffler Shop, Route 66 Insurance, etc.

Not long after Countryside, Joliet Road joins southbound I-55 (at exit 277), and you'll get funneled onto the interstate. Keep an eye on the signs that say "Route 66 use I-55."

A Route classic rears its red head in Willowbrook (exit 274 off I-55) shortly thereafter. **Dell Rhea's Chicken Basket** (630-325-0780), 645 Joliet Road at the intersection of I-55 and IL 83, has been frying bird for hungry travelers for decades. It's open Tues. through Thurs. 11 AM—9 PM, Fri. and Sat. 11 AM—10 PM, and Sun. 11 AM—9 PM. The location doesn't do much for nostalgia—it's behind a big, modern mall—but inside the juicy chicken is the real deal, along with homemade potato salad and baking-powder biscuits. Old men in trucker hats belly up at the attached cocktail lounge, where Sinatra and Dino impersonators croon standards. A four-piece chicken dinner costs $8.95.

Get back on I-55 and get off at exit 268 onto South Joliet Road, which becomes IL 53. It's industrial through Romeoville and beyond. In Joliet the road twists and turns through downtown's streets, but keep following I-55 South and you'll be on the right track.

The **Joliet Area Historical Museum and Route 66 Welcome Center** (815-723-5201; www.joliet museum.org), 204 North Ottawa Street, has some cool, free Route 66 exhibits as well as maps and brochures. It's open Mon. 9 AM—12 PM, Tues. through Sat. 10 AM—5pm, and Sun. 12 PM—5 PM. Paul McCartney stopped in summer 2008 to get oriented for his Route 66 road trip, so you know it's good stuff. Ask to see his signature on the guest log. And you can't leave town without detouring a few minutes north to pay your respects at the **Joliet Prison** (1125 Collins Street), of *Blues Brothers* fame. Fear not: the facility closed in 2004.

▪▪▪▪ WILMINGTON TO ODELL (50 MILES)

The road beyond Joliet holds more industrial corridors mixed with farmland.

The next sweet spot is Wilmington. When you hit town, follow IL 53 as it turns right onto Baltimore Street, and soon you'll spy the Gemini Giant—a 28-foot tall, 500-pound, pure-fiberglass spaceman who stands guard outside the **Launching Pad Drive-In** (815-476-6535), 810 East Baltimore Street. The burgers, chili dogs, fries, and shakes are so-so, but the photo opportunities are out of this world. It's open daily 10 AM—9:30 PM. Menu items cost $2—5.

In case you didn't get your fried-food fill, the **Polka Dot Drive-In** (815-458-3377), 222 North Front Street, pops up out of the farmland in Braidwood. Statues of Elvis, Betty Boop, James Dean, and Marilyn Monroe circle the '50s-style diner and enhance your chili-cheese fries experience. It's open daily 11 AM—9 PM. Menu items cost $2—5.

The Mother Road is easy to follow in this rural part of the state. Often Old Route 66 runs right alongside the highway. After a 25-mile stretch on the old beauty, it brings you to sleepy Odell and the well-preserved **Odell Service Station** (815-998-2133), 400 South West Street. This is a fantastic stop for photos, souvenirs, and a chat with the station's knowledgeable staff. They tell stories about how Odell once had 11 gas stations and so much traffic it had to dig a tunnel underneath Route 66 so local children could safely cross the street. It's usually open from 11 AM—3 PM. Admission is free.

South of Odell, alongside Old Route 66, are stretches of the true Great Diagonal Way, i.e., old slabs of the original pavement with grass tufts poking out.

▪▪▪▪ PONTIAC TO ATLANTA (60 MILES)

As you enter the town of Pontiac look for the **Old Log Cabin Inn** (815-842-2908), 18700 Old Route 66. When Route 66 was realigned, the restaurant was jacked up and rotated 180 degrees to face the new road. The down-home menu includes biscuits and gravy, ham and cheese melts, and pork tenderloins. It's open Mon. through Sat. 5 AM—8 PM. Breakfasts cost $3.50—6; sandwiches cost $3.50—7.

Pontiac is also home to the **Route 66 Hall of Fame** (815-844-4566; www.il66assoc.org), 110 Howard Street. Senior citizen volunteers staff the museum, located in an old fire station, and tend relics like the first Steak 'n Shake milkshake glasses, old license plates, and yellowed photos of roadsters. It's also the home of the Route 66 Association of Illinois, so it's a good place to get maps and info for onward travels. It's open Mon. through Fri. 11 AM—3 PM, and Sat. 10 AM—4 PM. Admission is free.

The road gets tricky to follow around the heavily populated twin towns of Bloomington-Normal, including an odd drive through a modern housing subdivision. Keep an eye out for the Route 66 signs, which do a decent job of reining you in.

About 12 miles beyond Bloomington stop off in Shirley and follow the signs to **Funk's Grove** (309-874-3360; www.funksmaple sirup.com), a 19th-century maple-syrup farm. Actually, it's sirup—with an "i"—which means the product is naturally sweet. When spelled with a "y" it means the makers have added fruit juice to enhance it. At Funk's they tap and boil the sirup from mid-February through mid-March, depending on the weather. And though it sounds like a sweet job, it takes 50 gallons of sap to make 1 gallon of sirup, so it ain't easy. The family sells their wares from a store on-site (free samples!); the sirup is usually available between March and August. Just down the road is the lovely Sugar Grove Nature Center, with trails and bird-watching as well as a brooding graveyard and chapel. Together, they make Funk's Grove a surprisingly impressive stop. Call for the farm's seasonal hours.

Next up: Paul Bunyan and his giant hot dog. The statue lords it over **Atlanta**, though Bunyan isn't native to the small town—Atlanta salvaged him from a Route 66 restaurant in Berwyn. Take Arch Street through town to see the big man, as well as the photo-worthy old-fashioned murals that cover Atlanta's brick walls.

▌▌▌▌ LINCOLN TO SPRINGFIELD (50 MILES)

Following Route 66 can be difficult from here on out. Try to stay on the frontage roads and watch for the brown route markers.

Lincoln is the only town named for Honest Abe while he was alive to appreciate it. It has an historic downtown dotted with lots of "Lincoln was here" plaques, along the lines of "Lincoln stood here" and "Lincoln spit watermelon seeds here" and "Lincoln once owned the building here." Abe practiced law at the **Postville Courthouse** (217-732-8930), 914 Fifth Street, now a state historic site and open for tours Tues.

Old gas pumps are a Route 66 staple, this one is in Funk's Grove.

through Sat. 12 PM–5 PM Mar. through Oct., and 12 PM–4 PM Nov. through Feb. Suggested donation is $2.

Broadwell lies about 10 miles down the road. The iconic **Pig Hip Restaurant** served up Route 66 lore through its museum, until a fire gutted it in 2007. The sign still stands, and the town is in the process of preserving whatever else it can.

It won't be long before you arrive in Springfield. The state capital has its own share of Route 66 sights, such as the **Cozy Dog Drive-In**—mythic birthplace of the corn dog—and **Shea's Gas Station Museum**. Springfield is also ground zero for Lincoln fanatics, who come to pay homage at his home, tomb, law office, and other sites. See chapter 14 ("Springfield's Abe Obsession") for details.

▪▪▪▪ GETTING THERE

The classic Route 66 road trip is made by car, of course. But it's also possible to do it on two wheels via the **Route 66 Bike Trail** (www.bikelib.org/route66). The League of Illinois Cyclists and Department of Natural Resources have produced a trail guide with detailed cue sheets, maps, suggestions of places to stay, and bike repair shops on each seg-

ment of the ride. The guide is available via download at the Web site or by calling 217-782-3715.

▪▪▪▪ WHERE TO STAY

You'll probably want to motor on down to Springfield, but the route does hold a couple of B&Bs if you want to bunk along the way.

Chester Manor (815-476-1055; www.chestermanor.net), 116 South Kankakee Street, Wilmington. This stately Italianate home decks out its four rooms with wrought-iron beds, thick drapes, and beautiful antiques. It's attached to a teahouse, which adds another touch of class. Rooms including breakfast cost $115–150 per night.

Three Roses B&B (815-844-3404; www.3rosesbnb.com), 209 East Howard Street, Pontiac. Be prepared for flowery. The four rooms have private bathrooms, but they're down the hall. There's free wireless Internet access. Rooms including full breakfast cost $120–140; it's $10 less per person if you stay sans breakfast.

▪▪▪▪ DON'T FORGET

The drive will be much smoother with good maps and materials to help guide you. See Resources, page 116, and get as much as you can ahead of time.

▮▮▮▮ SPECIAL EVENTS

Early September: Historic Route 66 Car Show (www.berwynrt66 .com). More than 400 classic cars turn up for this annual event on Ogden Avenue in Berwyn.

▮▮▮▮ RESOURCES

Route 66 Association of Illinois (815-844-4566; www.il66assoc .org). This is the same group that runs the Route 66 Hall of Fame in Pontiac. It has a clunky Web site, but a great free brochure titled *Exploring Route 66 in Illinois* that lists all the attractions along the road and their exit numbers off I-55.

Illinois Route 66 Heritage Project (866-378-7866; www .illinoisroute66.org). This non-governmental group is based out of Springfield and produces excellent free resources such as the *America's Byway: Illinois Route 66* brochure/map and *Route 66 Visitors Guide*.

Historic Route 66 (www .historic66.com/illinois). This privately run Web site provides detailed driving directions from sight to sight, and forums where you can post questions. It covers all the other states along Route 66, too.

National Historic Route 66 Federation (909-336-6131; www .national66.com). It sells maps and books that'll take you all the way to Los Angeles, baby.

14 • SPRINGFIELD'S ABE OBSESSION

Abraham Lincoln lived in Springfield from 1837 to 1861—from age 28 right up until he left for the White House to become the 16th president—and Springfield doesn't let you forget it. Abe mania has so overtaken the town it's easy to overlook this is also the Illinois state capital.

Are they milking Abe like a prize cow at the state fair? You bet. Here's the thing, though: it's *Lincoln,* one of history's most beloved and iconic figures, and Springfield counts his tomb, home, and presidential library and museum among its shrines. Nowhere on earth has such a large collection for Abe-o-philes to pay homage to.

The town can thank Lincoln for more than its tourist dollars. He's also the one who helped make it the state capital. Before he turned up, Springfield was just a ho-hum town on the prairie. After his arrival, he worked with eight legislator friends—known as the "Long Nine" since their aggregate height was 54 feet—to move the capital from sad little Vandalia, 77 miles to the south, to Springfield. It has remained the

government seat ever since.

Lincoln passed many milestones in Springfield. It's where he first practiced law and honed his political skills, got married, and had children. He sums it up best in his farewell address, which he gave when leaving for the White House: "Here I have lived a quarter of a century, and have passed from a young to an old man. Here my children have been born, and one is buried. I now leave, not knowing when or whether ever I may return." It proved prophetic, since the only time Lincoln returned was in a casket to be buried in Oak Ridge Cemetery.

A few Lincoln-free attractions pop up, including the Cozy Dog Drive-In and Shea's Gas Station Museum, a couple of Route 66 standbys. And remember that aforementioned state fair? It's here every August, so visitors can get their fill of butter cows and pig races.

Springfield rolls out the welcome mat year-round, although many places reduce their hours between November and May. The sheer number of tourist sites in the not-so-big town (population 111,400) amazes, and many of them are free or low cost. Food and lodging are economical, too, especially when compared to city prices.

▪▪▪▪ GETTING THERE

Springfield is 200 miles southwest of Chicago. Take I-55 south out of downtown, and it runs all the way to Springfield. Get off at exit 98B/IL 97 west (Clear Lake Avenue), and follow IL 97 for about 3 miles to reach Springfield's center. The trip takes about three and a half hours. You can also make the journey by way of Route 66; see chapter 13 for details.

Public transportation is also an option. **Amtrak** (800-872-7245; www.amtrak.com) runs four to five trains per day between Chicago and Springfield. The trip takes three and a half hours and costs $18–50 one way. Springfield's station is conveniently located downtown at the corner of 3rd and Washington Streets.

▪▪▪▪ GETTING AROUND

Most of the sights, restaurants, and hotels are easily walkable within the compact downtown. The Springfield Mass Transit District offers a "Historic Sites Bus" that makes a continual loop between the main Lincoln attrac-

tions Mon. through Sat. Cost is $1 per ride, $3 for a day pass.

▪▪▪▪ WHERE TO STAY

Statehouse Inn (217-528-5100; www.thestatehouseinn.com) 101 East Adams Street. Okay, so it's not the most attractive place from the outside. In fact, it's reminiscent of a drab Soviet apartment block. Inside, though, it's a different story—the hotel borders on swanky, particularly in the mod lobby bar. The rooms come equipped with comfy pillow-top mattresses, fluffy duvets, large granite-countertop bathrooms, and high-speed wired Internet access. Parking is free, and pets are welcome for an extra $25. Considering that it's located right across from the Capitol and walkable to everything else, the Statehouse is great value for the money. Rooms including hot breakfast buffet cost $95–145.

Inn at 835 (217-523-4466; www.innat835.com), 835 South 2nd Street. This turn-of-the-century, Arts and Crafts–style manor originally was designed for Miss Bell Miller, a florist who must have grown a money tree along with her daffodils. The 10 classy rooms—named after flowers (Iris, Poppy, Dahlia, etc.)—come in different sizes, with varying amenities like a Jacuzzi, private verandah, four-post bed, claw-foot bathtub, or combination thereof. All have private bathrooms and wired Internet access. There's free wine in the evening. The inn is at the southern edge of downtown, but within walking distance of all the sights. Rooms including full breakfast cost $125–175.

Hilton (217-789-1530; www .hilton.com), 700 East Adams Street. This 30-story concrete tower looks like something out of Homer Simpson's Springfield. It's usually filled with suits—not surprising since it's a full-service business hotel with all the requisite amenities, including a business center, fitness center, pool, and martini bar on the top floor. Alas, you have to pay for parking ($7 per night) and wireless access ($10.95 per day). Rooms including breakfast start at $145.

▮▮▮▮ CAMPING

Riverside Park (217-753-0630; www.springfieldparks.org), 4105 Sandhill Road (about 5 miles north of town, on the Sangamon River). Open mid-May through mid-Oct. It isn't the most beautiful or wooded campground, but it is one of the closest to town. There are 87 campsites (67 sites have water and electric hookups), along with hot showers and flush toilets. Campsites cost $10 for tents, $15 for RVs.

The corn-battered hot dog on a stick supposedly originated at the Cozy Dog Drive In, a Route 66 hot spot.

▮▮▮▮ EATING OUT

Cozy Dog Drive-In (217-525-1992), 2935 South 6th Street (about 3 miles south of downtown). Open Mon. through Sat. 8 AM–8 PM. Legend has it this small, unassuming snack shop birthed the corn dog—but be careful when ordering. "Saying 'corn dog' is like a cuss word," the guy at the counter explains. "We have *cozy* dogs. The special batter separates them from the pack." Actually, hot dogs on a stick taste the same no matter what you call them, but Cozy Dog is indeed a Route 66 hot spot, with all sorts of memorabilia and souvenirs in addition to its deep-fried foods. The location is unusual compared to other Route 66 stops, since it's on a busy, strip mall-lined street. Items, $2–4.

D'Arcy's Pint (217-492-8800), 661 West Stanford Avenue (about 3 miles south of downtown).

Open Mon. through Thurs. 11 AM—10 PM, Fri. and Sat. 11 AM—11 PM. This popular Irish pub serves a mean "horseshoe," Springfield's specialty sandwich that consists of fried meat on toasted bread, mounded with french fries and smothered in white-cheddar cheese sauce. If your arteries can't take the clogging, there's also a full menu of Irish dishes, including fried oysters, shepherd's pie, and fish and chips. Sandwiches, $6—8; mains, $9—12.

Maldaner's (217-522-4313), 222 South 6th Street. Open for lunch Mon. through Fri. 11 AM—2:30 PM, dinner Tues. through Thurs. 5 PM—9 PM, Fri. and Sat. 5 PM—10 PM. Classy, dark-wood Maldaner's has been around since 1884. Today, political types swirl martinis and broker deals over beef Wellington, veal meatballs, and pistachio-crusted salmon. The menu offers a couple of vegetarian pasta dishes, such as penne with locally grown asparagus. Dinner mains, $15—28.

Brewhaus (217-525-6399), 617 East Washington Street. Open daily afternoons and evenings. If you're looking for an after-dinner brewski downtown—say, a booth to decompress in after the day's Abe-a-thon—this straightforward watering hole provides a decent beer selection.

▉ ▉ ▉ ▉ LINCOLN SIGHTS

Lincoln Home (217-492-4150; www.nps.gov/liho), corner of 8th and Jackson Streets. Open daily 8:30 AM—5 PM. Abe and Mary Lincoln lived in this abode from 1844 until they moved to the White House in 1861. To visit, you must pick up a ticket next door at the National Park Service visitors center (426 South 7th Street), and then enter with a ranger on one of the 25-minute tours. The rangers tell engaging stories, and you'll learn tidbits such as how Lincoln arrived in Springfield $1,500 in debt, on a borrowed horse, and carrying all his worldly belongings in two saddlebags. After the tour, you can check out the rest of the block. The whole street has been preserved, and a couple of structures are open to visitors. Busloads of school kids start flooding in around 10 AM, so arrive earlier to avoid crowds. History buffs should browse the book selection in the visitors center. Site admission is free.

Lincoln Presidential Library and Museum (217-558-8844; www.alplm.org), 212 North 6th Street. Open daily 9 AM—5 PM. "The museum will literally knock your socks off," the park ranger at the Lincoln Home (see above) promises. He isn't kidding, as your socks do ripple during the 20-minute, surround-sound film that tells Lincoln's life story. Cannons explode and smoke fills the room—all part of the special effects onslaught that makes history exciting here. A couple of exhibits are over-the-top Disney

The Lincoln-Herndon Law Offices where Abe practiced for several years before becoming president.

Abe Lincoln and his wax family welcome visitors to the Presidential Museum.

(i.e., the hologram Ghosts of the Library). But overall the museum does a bang-up job detailing Lincoln's life and putting it in Civil War context. The museum contains the world's biggest collection of Lincoln artifacts, everything from his Gettysburg Address and Emancipation Proclamation to his shaving mirror and briefcase. Unfortunately, the famed documents are only occasionally on display given their frailty. Allow at least two hours to see the whole shebang. The library across the street is more for scholars than tourists, but you're welcome to stroll in. Admission costs $10 for adults, $4 for children.

Lincoln's Tomb, in Oak Ridge Cemetery (217-782-2717), a few miles north of downtown on Monument Avenue. Open daily 9 AM—5 PM Mar. 1 through Oct. 31, 9 AM—4 PM Nov. 1 through Feb. 28. After his assassination, Lincoln's body was returned to Springfield, where it lies today in an impressive, skyscraping monument. Visitors circle through the burial chamber inside, past the crypts of three of Lincoln's four sons and his wife Mary. When you come to Abe's marker, remember this: his body is actually 13 feet below floor level, with a six-foot concrete slab on top of the coffin to discourage grave robbers.

Outside, visitors can walk around the monument and get up close and personal with Lincoln's bust. His shiny nose, which visitors rub for good luck, shows how many people come to pay their respects here. Admission is free.

Old State Capitol (217-785-7960), corner of 5th and Adams Streets. Open daily 9 AM—5 PM mid-Apr. through early Sept., Tues. through Sat. only the rest of the year. Knowledgeable and chatty docents will take you through the wonderfully preserved building and reveal more Lincoln stories and trivia than you ever thought possible. Here Lincoln tried cases before the Supreme Court, gave his famous "House Divided" speech, and lay in state after his assassination (makeup and heavy perfume required, since the body arrived from the East Coast after a 12-day train journey). Suggested donation is $4.

Lincoln-Herndon Law Offices (217-785-7960), corner of 6th and Adams Streets. Open daily 9 AM—5 PM mid-Apr. through early Sept., Tues. through Sat. only the rest of the year. Lincoln practiced law in this office with partner William Herndon for more than 15 years. Most of the furnishings are reproductions. Admission is by way of the 20-minute guided tour. Suggested donation is $4.

Lincoln's Ghost Walk (217-525-1825; www.springfieldwalks .com), corner of 6th and Adams Streets (by the Lincoln family statues). Held Tues. through Sat. 7:30 PM, Mar. 1 through Nov. 1. Swing by downtown's Lincoln sites and hear the spooky, séance-filled tales surrounding his life and death. The group also offers three other themed tours, but the ghost walk remains the most popular. Buy tickets at the Tinsley Dry Goods store (209 South 6th Street). The 90-minute tours cost $12 for adults, $8 for children.

▮▮▮▮ NON-LINCOLN SIGHTS

Shea's Gas Station Museum (217-522-0475), 2075 Peoria Road. Open Tues. through Fri. 8 AM—4 PM, Sat. 8 AM—12 PM. Crusty Bill Shea, an octogenarian former gas station owner who still dons blue coveralls, and his son take you on a lengthy tour of this small cluttered "museum." While they have several pieces of Route 66 memorabilia, they also have loads of personal items on display, such as artifacts from when Bill fought in WW2. Be prepared to spend at least 30 minutes being walked through all of it in detail. Outside, the shiny Route 66 pumps and signs provide great photo opportunities. Admission costs $2.

▪▪▪▪ MARY'S MADNESS

Mary Todd Lincoln, Abe's wife, took a public relations thrashing like few other first ladies. Critics attacked her as a spendthrift when she used public funds to pretty up the White House. They said she was a Confederate spy, since two of her younger brothers and a brother-in-law were killed fighting for the Confederacy (her family was from Kentucky, where loyalties were split). Abe's Springfield law partner William Herndon started the rumor that she was a second-choice wife for Abe, and that he really loved a woman named Ann Rutledge, who died early on.

But worst of all was when Mary's oldest son, Robert, had her declared insane and committed to an asylum. She was 57 years old and suffering the aftereffects of watching three of her four sons die, and her husband shot while sitting at her side. She continued to spend money wildly—it's said she walked around Chicago with $56,000 in government bonds sewn into her petticoats—and son Robert used that as part of the prosecution.

The trial was an international sensation. Few people paid attention a year later when the court set the verdict aside and declared her sane. Mary lived out most of her remaining years in Europe.

The Lincoln Home bookshop has several books on Mary and her madness, which today might be categorized as bipolar disorder.

Route 66 Drive-In (217-698-0066; www.route66-drivein.com), 1700 Recreation Drive (Exit 93 off I-72). It screens first-run flicks under the stars in summertime. Tickets cost $6 for adults, $3 for children.

Dana-Thomas House (217-782-6776; www.dana-thomas.org), 301 East Lawrence Street. Open Wed. through Sun. 9 AM–4 PM. As this book was going to press, the fate of the Dana-Thomas House—a pristine, 1904 Prairie-style home that Frank Lloyd Wright built for a wealthy local socialite—was up in the air. The state government had targeted it for closure due to budget cutbacks. Call before planning your visit. If the house stays open, the hour-long tour will thrill Wright fans. Mrs. Dana gave Wright a "blank check" to design the 35-room, 12,000-square-foot spread, and it contains a huge collection of original

Wright art glass and furniture. Suggested donation is $5.

Illinois State Capitol (217-782-2099), intersection of 2nd Street and Capitol Avenue. Tours Mon. through Fri. 9 AM—4 PM, Sat. and Sun. 9 AM—3 PM. When the legislature is in session, visitors can get a firsthand view of sparring lawmakers and where all those taxes originate. The tours are free.

Museum of Funeral Customs (217-544-3480; www.funeral museum.org), 1440 Monument Avenue. Open Tues. through Sat. 10 AM—4 PM, Sun. 1 PM—4 PM. It's an intriguing concept, but this one-room museum is pretty tame. Casket displays and explanatory placards about the "Pioneers of Embalming" are as exciting as it gets. Admission costs $4.

▌▌▌▌ SPECIAL EVENTS

Mid-August: Illinois State Fair (www.illinoisstatefair.info). The two-week extravaganza offers corn dogs, butter cows, high dive shows, and pig races at the fairgrounds north of downtown.

Late September: International Route 66 Mother Road Festival (www.route66fest.com). Vintage cars, Elvis impersonators, and corn dogs take over downtown's streets for three days.

2009 marks Lincoln's 200th birthday, and Springfield will host several additional events

throughout the year in honor of the occasion.

▌▌▌▌ NEARBY

Lincoln's New Salem State Historic Site (217-632-4000; www .lincolnsnewsalem.com), on IL 97 in Petersburg, 20 miles northwest of Springfield. Open Wed. through Sun. 9 AM—5 PM. In 1831, before he moved to Springfield, Lincoln lived in the frontier village of New Salem, where he cycled through gigs as a clerk, storekeeper, and postmaster while beginning his law studies. The site reconstructs the village with building replicas, historical displays, and costumed performances. Suggested donation is $4 for adults, $2 for children.

▌▌▌▌ RESOURCES

Springfield Convention and Visitors Bureau (800-545-7300; www.visitspringfieldillinois.com), 109 North 7th Street. Open Mon. through Fri. 8:30 AM—5 PM. The Visitors Guide has a useful town map.

Looking for Lincoln Heritage Coalition (217-782-6817; www .lookingforlincoln.com). Provides the lowdown on Abe sites, not just in Springfield, but throughout central Illinois. Go online or call for a hard copy of the chock-full *Looking for Lincoln* booklet.

15 • QUAD CITIES UNCOVERED

Who knew? A trip to the Quad Cities, and you return a well-rounded connoisseur of art, history, and culture.

Four towns comprise the Quads: Moline and Rock Island in Illinois, and their twins Davenport and Bettendorf in Iowa. The churning Mississippi River divides the two states.

Art education comes from the Figge Museum, a superb facility that would be at home in a metropolis 10 times the Q.C.'s size. Beyond the permanent collection of Grant Wood cornscapes and Haitian voodoo art, traveling exhibits take in themes from psychedelic pop art to Da Vinci paintings to wood-carved duck decoys. It's always an enlightening mishmash.

Rock Island's Civil War—era arsenal and P.O.W. camp provide good history lessons. As for culture, jazz fans know Bix Beiderbecke tooted his horn in Davenport, and every July Bix-heads flock here for the Jazz Fest. The region also has long been a way station where blues, country, and other traditional "roots music" met and mixed before moving upriver. Davenport's Redstone Building tells the tale from yesteryear and hosts daily concerts and music workshops today.

Just to keep your head spinning, the Quad Cities offer eagle watching in winter on the Mississippi's shores, and farm rigs year-round at the John Deere Pavilion. You can snooze in an old Carmelite monastery or in Bix Beiderbecke's grandparents' pad.

The Q.C.—not to be confused with Southern California's O.C.— are certainly not glamorous. But if you like to poke around and discover cultural tidbits, this is a worthy getaway.

▮▮▮▮ GETTING THERE

The Quad Cities are 160 miles west of Chicago. Take I-55 south out of downtown. After 40 miles or so, merge onto I-80 west (near Joliet). This will take you all the way to the Q.C.'s outskirts. From there, follow I-280/I-74 west, then stay on I-74 west, which runs to downtown Moline or on into Bettendorf, Iowa.

You can also reach the Quad Cities via I-290 west from downtown, and then merge onto I-88 west, a.k.a. the Ronald Reagan Memorial Tollway, which goes straight to the Q.C. However, it'll cost you $5 in tolls, and it's typically the same amount of driving time. The trip takes just under three hours.

■■■■ GETTING AROUND

In summer the **Channel Cat Water Taxi** (309-788-3360; www.qcmetrolink.com) zips across the Mississippi River between Moline (including the John Deere Pavilion), Bettendorf (17th Street and Isle Parkway), and East Davenport (foot of Mound Street). The boat runs daily from Memorial Day to Labor Day and cycles through the stops at least once per hour; it runs on weekends only in September. A day pass costs $6 for adults, $3 for children; bike transport is free.

■■■■ WHERE TO STAY

Abbey Hotel (563-355-0291, 800-438-7535; www.theabbeyhotel.com), 1401 Central Avenue, Bettendorf. Just think: your big sweet room used to be divided into five smaller rooms housing five nuns. And instead of having niceties like marble bathrooms and cable TV, they had straw mattresses. This was a Carmelite nunnery until 1975, and you can see how severely the sisters lived via a room that's been preserved

on the third floor. Those days are over, and the 19-room inn today offers cushy beds, big bathrooms, in-room wireless access, and Mississippi River views from the upper-floor rooms. The good-value Abbey is located in the middle of a residential neighborhood, up on a bluff—just look for the building with the crosses and statuary on top. Rooms including continental breakfast cost $100–140.

Beiderbecke B&B (563-323-0047, 866-300-8858; www.bbonline.com/ia/beiderbecke), 532 West 7th Street, Davenport. This 19th-century, Stick-style manor belonged to jazzman Bix Beiderbecke's grandparents. The four guest rooms are heaped with Victorian antiques, including porcelain pitchers and washbasins, brass and walnut beds, and claw-foot tubs. Each room has a private bathroom. The Tower and Mississippi Rose rooms also have views of the Mississippi River. Kids are welcome, but pets aren't. Rooms including full breakfast cost $85–105.

Stoney Creek Inn (309-743-0101, 800-659-2220; www.stoneycreekinn.com), 101 18th Street, Rock Island. The hotel's 140 rooms are average quality, and it goes a bit over the top with the woodsy theme, but it's a good bang for the buck given the freebies: continental breakfast, in-room wireless access, indoor and outdoor pools, a whirlpool, and exercise room. The riverfront location is also a perk: it's a third of a mile from the John Deere Pavilion, two-thirds of a mile from the Rock Island Arsenal, and the River Trail for hiking and biking is practically in the backyard. Families can opt for rooms with a set of log bunk beds. The flip side of the hotel's family-friendliness is that noise from slamming doors and kids running the hallways can be an issue. Stoney Creek is a regional chain. Rooms including continental breakfast cost $100–135.

Sleep in the family home of Jazz Age hero Bix Beiderbecke.

Davenport's Abbey Hotel has carved unique rooms out of an old nunnery.
PHOTOGRAPH BY LISA BERAN

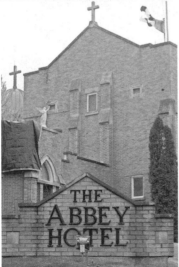

■■■■ CAMPING

West Lake Park (563-328-3281; www.scottcountyiowa.com /conservation), 14910 100th Avenue, Davenport (about 15 miles west of town). Open year-round. The park has three campgrounds, including one at Buffalo Shore with views of the Mississippi River. Sites range from primitive with just a fire ring and picnic table, to full electric and water hookups for RVs. Everyone shares the hot showers and flush toilets. The campgrounds are in a lake-filled recreation area where locals boat, fish, and swim. Campsites cost $11–18.

■■■■ EATING OUT

Mojo's Cafe (563-326-1333), 129 North Main Street, Davenport. Open Mon. through Fri. 7 AM–9 PM, Sat. 10 AM–9 PM. Located on the first floor of the Redstone Building, Mojo's makes an ideal quick-bite stop after art-gazing at the Figge (see What to See and Do, below). The café serves soups and sandwiches named after musical performers, like the Aretha Franklin C-a-p-r-e-s-e (mozzarella, tomatoes, and basil), Dick Dale Big Kahuna Tuna, and Buck Owens Chicken Pickin Salad. Local musicians and poets hang out here, and there are usually free concerts at lunchtime, as well as open mics, jam sessions, and more concerts in the evenings. Soups and sandwiches, $4–6.

Lagomarcino's (563-324-6137), 2132 East 11th Street, Davenport. Open daily 9 AM–5 PM. *Roadfood* authors Michael and Jane Stern praised this old-fashioned ice cream parlor as having "the best hot fudge in this solar system or any other," as Lagomarcino's proudly advertises. The fudge isn't thick but has nice caramel-y undertones. Lagomarcino's also makes chocolate truffles and other candies on-site, and you'll see them bring out fresh trays for the front display case (which you must stand by and sniff while paying your bill, so we don't have to tell you what happens next). There's also a small menu of soups and sandwiches including ham salad, tuna melts, and BLTs, and seating is at the counter or in booths. Soups and sand-

wiches, $4–6; sundaes, $3.55–4.25.

Trattoria Tiramisu (563-323-2787), 1804 State Street, Bettendorf. Open for lunch Mon. through Fri. 11 AM–2 PM, for dinner Mon. through Thurs. 5 PM–9 PM, Fri. and Sat. 5 PM–10 PM. Cute Tiramisu plays the trattoria role well, with candlelit tables, mural-painted walls, and wine bottles galore. Italian staples fill the big menu—pastas, chicken, veal, and seafood dishes—and they arrive in giant portions. Mains, $11–18.

▪▪▪▪ WHAT TO SEE AND DO

Most sights are concentrated in downtown Davenport, at the offshore Rock Island Arsenal, and at the John Deere Pavilion in downtown Moline.

Arts: The **Figge Art Museum** (563-326-7804; www.figgeart museum.org), 225 West 2nd Street, Davenport, is fab. Open Tues. through Sun. 10 AM–5 PM, to 9 PM Thurs. You'll scratch your head in wonderment at how such a world-class institution landed in wee Iowa. The permanent collection includes a room devoted to Iowa native Grant Wood and three rooms of colorful Haitian art. Two of the four floors are devoted to changing exhibits, where you can look at, say, glass-

The fab Figge Art Museum hangs an eye-popping collection.

works or African wood carvings or Henry Moore tapestries—all thought-provoking and somewhat offbeat. The Figge is big enough to absorb an afternoon, yet small enough to manage in a single visit (unlike the Art Institute of Chicago, which can feel overwhelming). Bonus: the museum's glassy exterior provides views of the Mississippi River. Admission costs $7 for adults, $4 for children.

Roots music: "Roots music" is the broad term given to folk, blues, traditional country, and other genres that originated with and told the stories of ordinary people in everyday communities, mostly in the South. As a transportation hub on the Mississippi River, the Quad Cities became a crossroads for roots music. The multiuse **Redstone Building** (563-326-1333; www.rivermusic experience.org), 129 North Main Street in Davenport, tells the story. Open Mon. through Fri. 7 AM—9 PM, Sat. 10 AM—9 PM. Exhibits on the second floor explain the different kinds of river roots music and provide headphones to listen to the St. Louis style (epitomized by Ike and Tina Turner), Memphis style (B.B. King was the main man), and Delta style, among others. You can also poke around old recording studios. To hear roots music live, there's the **Redstone Room** (www .redstoneroom.com), a 250-seat venue that books top regional and national acts, such as Alejandro Escovedo and Junior Brown. Mojo's Cafe (see Eating Out, page 127) is on the building's first floor and offers more live music. A community drum circle ($5) bangs away the last Saturday of every month. Exhibit admission is free.

Jazz music: Besides roots music, the region's other noted draw is **Bix Beiderbecke**, the man with the golden cornet. Born and buried in Davenport, Bix was a self-taught hero of the Jazz Age who influenced everyone from Louis Armstrong to Miles Davis. He died at age 28 of alcohol-related complications, but his legacy was sealed. Bix-o-philes—and there are masses of them—descend on Davenport annually for the Memorial Jazz Fest that includes a concert at Bix's gravesite (see Special Events, page 132). For fans who want to see Bix-related places of interest, the visitors center provides a photocopied page of "Bix Sites" with a map. The most prominent is his birthplace at 1934 Grand Avenue; the off-white Victorian home is privately owned, but a plaque by the front door lets you know you've got the right place. Another site is the Beiderbecke B&B (see Where to Stay, page 126), which was his grandparents' home.

Hiking and biking: The Quad Cities unfurl more than 60 miles of hike/bike trails. The grand dame is the River Trail, part of the larger **Mississippi River Trail** (www.mississippirivertrail.org) that runs the length of the waterway from Minnesota to Louisiana. The Q.C. visitors center (see Resources, page 132) has trail maps, and you can hop on the path right outside the building. The visitors center also rents bikes, tandems, and kids' trailers, though you might want to call ahead to see what's in stock. Rentals are available Apr. 1 through Nov. 1 and cost $7 per hour or $28 per day.

For riders looking to go farther on the path in Illinois, the League of Illinois Cyclists and Department of Natural Resources have produced a trail guide with detailed cue sheets, maps, suggestions of places to stay, and bike repair shops on each segment of the ride. A good section goes north to Galena (see chapter 17). The guide is available via download (www.bikelib.org/mrt) or by calling 217-782-3715.

River views: The 50-foot **Skybridge** in Davenport looks kind of gaudy, but it does provide great views of Old Man River through its glass walls and glass elevator. Enter via the courtyard on 2nd Street, next to the Redstone Building. If you walk over the bridge, you'll end up across River Drive by LeClaire Park. Admission is free.

Antique shopping: The browsable Village of East Davenport, where Lagomarcino's is located (see Eating Out, page 128), is filled with old-timey storefronts that hold delis, coffee shops, bars, and cool specialty shops. Good pickins are also available 14 miles upriver in the small town of LeClaire, Iowa, where antique shops cluster on Cody Road.

Rock Island Arsenal: A 3-mile island floats in the Mississippi River just offshore from the town of Rock Island, and it holds several points of interest. It's also an active U.S. Army facility, so all visitors over age 16 must bring a photo I.D. to enter. The **Rock Island Arsenal Museum** (309-782-5021; www.ria.army.mil), open Tues. through Sun. 10 AM–4 PM, showcases an impressive small arms collection amassed over the years since the arsenal was established in 1862. There are two cemeteries on the island: a **national cemetery** with more than 23,000 gravestones—it's one of the largest and oldest in the country—and a **Civil War–era prisoner-of-war cemetery** with more than 1,900 gravestones from December 1863 through July 1865. The **Mississippi River Visitor Center** (309-794-5338; www.miss river.org), open daily 9 AM–5 PM, provides up-close views to see barge pilots maneuvering through Lock and Dam 15. Rangers provide tours on summer weekends at 11 AM and 2 PM. In winter, especially from January through mid-February, the visitor center is a prime eagle-viewing location. Admission is free to each of the sites.

Tractor ogling: Get your farm machinery fix at the **John Deere Pavilion** (309-765-1000; www .johndeereattractions.com), 1400 River Drive, Moline. Open Mon. through Fri. 9 AM–5 PM, Sat. 10 AM–5 PM, Sun. 12 PM–4 PM. Displays of vintage and modern equipment—including lots and lots of tractors—stuff the copper-and-glass building. The Deere store is next door and the place to get green-colored gear such as the revered trucker hat. Deere's international headquarters is not on-site, but rather a few miles southeast. To see where John Deere lived and worked as a blacksmith before he struck it rich, check out chapter 19. Admission is free.

■ ■ ■ ■ HISTORIC SITES

Black Hawk State Historic Site (309-788-0177; www.blackhawk park.org), 1510 46th Avenue, Rock Island. Open daily dawn–10 PM. More than just a "site," this is a 208-acre forested park with 4 miles of hiking trails by the Rock River. More than 175 bird species (including eagles in winter) hang out in the woods, which is said to be one of the least disturbed patches of nature in Illinois. The Hauberg Indian Museum is in Watch Tower Lodge and tells the story of Sauk leader Black Hawk and his people. Alas, proposed government cutbacks at press time might result in the museum's closure, so call before planning a visit. Admission is free.

■ ■ ■ ■ SPECIAL EVENTS

Mid-January: Quad Cities Bald Eagle Days (www.missriver.org), Rock Island. Food, art, and an environmental fair supplement eagle viewings.

Early July: Mississippi Valley Blues Festival (www.mvbs.org), Davenport. National and regional blues acts wail at LeClaire Park on the Mississippi River.

Late July: Bix Beiderbecke Memorial Jazz Fest (www.bix society.org) and Bix 7 Run (www .bix7.com), Davenport. Four days of traditional jazz shows, jam sessions, and a graveside concert in honor of the local 1920s jazz legend. The run occurs on Sat. of fest weekend and takes a huffing, puffing route up Davenport's hills; it attracts elite runners from around the country, as well as novices.

▪▪▪▪ RESOURCES

Quad Cities Visitors Center (563-322-3911, 800-747-7800; www .visitquadcities.com), 102 South Harrison Street, Davenport. Open Mon. through Fri. 9 AM–5 PM year-round, plus Sat. 10 AM–4 PM in summer. Located in an old river-front train depot, this well-stocked facility has hiking/biking trail maps, Bix Beiderbecke site info, Great River Road driving info, and bike rentals. There's another riverfront outlet in Moline at 1601 River Drive.

CHILL

16 • FAST BREAK:
Chicago Botanic Garden

You need to unwind, escape from the city to a piney forest or flower-jumbled prairie. Hear the splatter of a waterfall or gurgling creek to clear your mind. But damn, time is tight and there's no way you'll be able to get to Starved Rock, the Rock River Valley, or any of those other chill-worthy places.

Panic not. The Chicago Botanic Garden blooms year-round in Glencoe, 25 miles north of the city, and it has the requisite forest, prairie, and waterfall. The 385 acres hold lakes, rivers, nine islands, 10 bridges, and 2.3 million plants to boot.

It's easy enough to zip to the garden by car or train. Those who have the time and inclination—and muscled legs—can make a full day of it biking here via the North Branch Trail (propelled by a Superdawg!). No matter how you arrive, you'll want to partake of the garden's free cooking classes, how-to-grow demonstrations, and weekend festival lineup.

▐▐▐▐ GETTING THERE

By car, take I-90/94 west from downtown, and follow I-94 west when it splits off. I-94 eventually merges with US 41; follow signs for the latter from here onward. Exit at Lake Cook Road, and travel a half mile east to the garden. The trip takes 30 minutes.

Metra trains also run here via the Union Pacific North Line. On weekends, take the train to Glencoe, where a free trolley awaits and shuttles visitors to the garden. On weekdays, or if you enjoy a brisk walk, take the train to Braeside and stroll a mile east on Lake Cook Road (a.k.a. County Line Road) to reach the grounds.

For the scenic, slowpoke driving route, head all the way up on Sheridan Road, a ribbon that curves through the mansion-studded communities of Evanston, Wilmette, Kenilworth, and Winnetka.

To reach the Botanic Garden on two wheels, see the North Branch Bike Trek sidebar, page 136.

▪▪▪▪ EATING OUT

Garden Cafe (847-835-3040). Open daily 8 AM—4 PM; hours change seasonally and are extended in warmer months. The café prepares a groovy little meal and tries to use local ingredients when possible. Omelets and organic coffee hit the tables for breakfast. Arugula-and-goat-cheese flatbread pizza, hot and cold sandwiches, garlic parmesan fries, and even a small sushi selection make up the lunchtime menu. Free wireless access is available while you munch. Breakfast, $4—5; mains, $5.50—7.

▪▪▪▪ WHAT TO SEE AND DO

Stop in the visitor center by the parking lot to pick up a garden map and schedule of the day's events. Then take your pick of foliage from 26 settings. Among the highlights are the **Prairie, Japanese Garden**, and **Rose Garden**. And don't keep your eyes on the ground, because up in the trees 255 bird species flutter. Even if you're not a bird-watcher, it's totally impressive to see a hawk swoop in and hover a few yards away on a tree branch. Or to see a yellow-rumped warbler (because it's just fun to say). For details on the garden's winged residents, check www.chicago botanic.org/birds.

If you're visiting on the weekend, you'll likely have a choice of free classes to attend. The **Garden Chef Series** takes place on Sat. and Sun. at 1:30 PM and 2:30 PM from late May through early Oct. Local cooks from restaurants like Tru, Wishbone, and Lula Cafe give demonstration classes using garden produce. The classes occur in

The North Branch Trail rolls through forest preserves for 20 miles from the city to the Chicago Botanic Garden.

▮▮▮▮ THE NORTH BRANCH BIKE TREK

Riding your bike to the Botanic Garden is a journey all its own. The North Branch Trail paves the way—literally. The flat asphalt path starts in the city on the northwest corner of Devon and Caldwell Avenues (about 5600 west). From there you pedal north along the Chicago River through a series of wooded forest preserves. The most scenic part is toward the end when you reach the Skokie Lagoons, seven interconnected watering holes where locals kayak, canoe, and fish for bass and walleye. The Botanic Garden sprouts up shortly thereafter—a trek of about 20 miles one way.

It's a dandy ride through lots of tree-shaded green space, and for long stretches you'll feel like you're far from the city. Then—buzz kill—the trail dumps out onto a main street like Oakton or Dempster, where you must wait for the traffic light and cross a car-jammed intersection. Soon enough, though, you're back in the woods pedaling away.

The forest preserves offer several picnic groves and bathrooms along the route. Other than that, you're on your own—which means you need either to bring your own food and drink or fuel up ahead of time.

We suggest the former. Is it mere coincidence that **Superdawg** (773-763-0660), 6363 North Milwaukee Avenue, lies near the trailhead? Or was it meant to be, like the love shared by Mr. and Mrs. Dawg—a pair of giant, neon, fiberglass weenies—atop the eatery's roof?

Encased meat aficionados say Superdawg serves the best hot dog in Chicago. It's certainly a sight to behold, with the pure beef weenie lovingly set upon a bed of Superfries in a red box "bed." Super

the open amphitheater in the Regenstein Fruit and Vegetable Garden.

The Fruit and Vegetable Garden also hosts free **Weekend Family Drop-In Activities** from II AM–4 PM during the same months. Kids and parents can join in projects to learn how their favorite foods grow, how roots form, and how bees pollinate flowers, among other activities.

Remember those aforementioned 2.3 million plants? Each one is named, mapped, and recorded. The Botanic Garden is a burgers, Supershakes, and a few other Superfoods round out the menu. Carhops deliver the goods to your vehicle—the way things used to be when the drive-in stand opened in 1948—or you can go inside to order and then eat at the picnic tables.

From the North Branch trailhead, ride just past the 1-mile marker. Here the trail splits. You can bear right and stay on the trail, or go left and ride until you come out through the Caldwell Woods parking lot by Milwaukee and Devon Avenues. Superdawg sits at the intersection's southeast corner. The Caldwell parking lot is also a good place to leave the car and start the trail if you're driving your bike here.

Superdawg is open Sun. through Thurs. 11 AM–1 AM, Fri. and Sat. 11 AM–2 AM. Hot dogs and burgers, $4.75–6.50.

Another nearby fueling stop is **Chocolate Shoppe Ice Cream** (773-763-9778), 5337 West Devon Avenue. It scoops 32 flavors of "super premium Wisconsin goodness," as the saying goes, and it's three blocks east of the North Branch trailhead. When the ride gets tough, focusing on the dreamy Zanzibar Dark Chocolate ice cream or refreshing raspberry-lemon ice can pull you through. The shop is open daily 10 AM–11 PM. Single scoop, $3.15; double scoop, $4.50.

Finally, if you want to make the trek but don't have a bike, rentals are available at **Edgebrook Cycle & Sport** (773-792-1669), 6450 North Central Avenue. The bikes are kind of cruddy and service isn't particularly friendly, but it's just a few blocks from the trailhead—and it's your only choice in the area. The shop is open Mon., Tues., Thurs., and Fri. 10 AM–8 PM, Sat. 9 AM–5 PM, Sun. 11 AM–4 PM. Rentals cost $9 per hour with a two-hour minimum; helmets and locks are *not* provided.

real-deal research institution, affiliated with Northwestern University through the 38,000-square-foot **Conservation Science Center**. At the time of writing, the center was still being built, but it's slated for completion in 2009. Part of the new facility will be open to visitors, so you'll be able to see microscope-wielding scientists in action as they suss out matters like fungal diversity.

Be prepared to walk during your visit. It's 2.6 miles around the Botanic Garden's oval-shaped perimeter, and 1 mile from the entrance to the farthest garden (the Prairie).

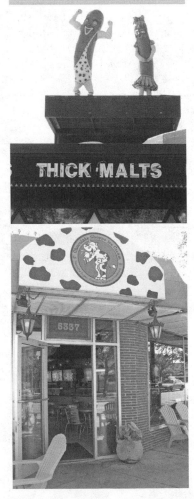

Superdawg, near the North Branch trailhead, serves some of Chicago's best weenies.

Also nearby is Chocolate Shoppe, which scoops dreamy ice cream.

Admission costs $15 per car. It's free if you come by bike.

▮▮▮▮ SPECIAL EVENTS

Contact the Botanic Garden (847-835-5440; www.chicagobotanic.org/calendar) for more information on these and other events:

Mid-May: A Bloomin' Sale. Plot your home garden, choosing from the 40,000 plants on offer here, including unusual varieties and native wildflowers.

Early June: Wine Festival. Tastings from more than 200 global vintners, as well as wine seminars and cooking demonstrations with local chefs and sommeliers.

Mid-August: Kite Festival. A family event, with kite-making workshops, kite-launch competitions, and stunts by pro fliers.

Early October: Bulb Bazaar. Buy your daffodils, tulips, hyacinth, trout lilies, and other specialty bulbs.

▮▮▮▮ RESOURCES

Chicago Botanic Garden (847-835-5440; www.chicagobotanic.org), 1000 Lake Cook Road, Glencoe. Open daily 8 AM—dusk.

Forest Preserve District of Cook County (www.fpdcc.com). Download the North Trail bike map (click "Recreation," then "Bicycling," then "North Branch Trail System").

17 • GO WITH THE FLOW IN GALENA

Galena takes a beating from many urbanites, chided as a place for the "newlywed and nearly dead." Fair enough: seniors and handholding couples *are* here en masse, as are antique and fudge shops in quantities that'll make your head explode.

But fear not. All that hullabaloo huddles on a six-block stretch of Main Street. And if it's not your scene, it's easy enough to leave behind to bike, kayak, drive along old stagecoach trails, or pick blueberries and take cooking classes at local organic farms. When the winds shift and snow falls, you can ski and snowshoe, too.

Young and old, shoppers and kayakers do all agree on one thing: Galena's setting is gorgeous. The town spreads across wooded hillsides near the Mississippi River in the northwest corner of Illinois. Farms dotted with cows, red barns, and silvery silos surround it. And Civil War—era streets and mansions time-warp you into a vanished era.

In the mid-19th century, the industrial demands of the United States, spurred on by the Civil War, sparked Galena into one of the Midwest's richest river towns. Lead was the name of the game. It bestowed Galena with its moniker ("galena" is the scientific term for lead sulfide ore) and funded the mighty redbrick manors that shot up throughout town. Then the lead ran out, railroads replaced rivers as the primary mode of transportation, and a few years after the war Galena began its spiral into a century-long funk.

The town was so poor and neglected it never even bothered to tear down its abandoned buildings. Which, of course, turned out to be its salvation. Folks drifted back in during the 1960s and began restoring the houses and shops. Galena's charm today comes from it looking almost identical to its 150-year-old self. You can almost imagine Ulysses S. Grant—the nation's 18th president and Galena's most famous resident—prowling the streets looking for a cocktail, and women in hoop skirts entertaining in their elegant homes (which they do today, too, only the homes are now B&Bs, and they've

Gourmet restaurants, antique shops, and galleries line long, curving Main Street.

ditched the skirts).

Several historic sites and rich architecture bear out the town's one-time importance. The Grant Home and Belvedere Mansion top the list, though all you have to do is walk down Main Street or climb the steep stairs to Prospect Street to see more Greek Revival, Italianate, Gothic Revival, and Queen Anne structures.

By now you're thinking to heck with history. Let's move on to the great outdoors. Local outfitters can set you up to canoe, kayak, bike, or bird-watch nearby along the Galena River and the Mississippi River backwaters. Or head farther afield, where there are parks and resorts galore. Mississippi Palisades, Apple River Canyon, and Chestnut Mountain all lie within a half-hour drive and provide spots to hike, camp, rock climb, and ski.

Back in town, there's always Main Street. After all, antiques and fudge do have their merits. Art galleries, bead stores, gourmet food purveyors, and clothing boutiques also manage to squeeze in on the long curving road, as do most of Galena's restaurants.

So forgive Galena its touristy sins. Underneath the puff lies a genuine little town whose beauty relaxes and recharges the batteries.

▪▪▪▪ GETTING THERE

Galena is 165 miles northwest of Chicago. Take I-90 west out of the city (tolls apply). Just before Rockford, follow I-39 and US 51 heading south for 3 miles, and then merge onto US 20 west, which runs all the way into Galena. The trip takes about three hours.

▪▪▪▪ GETTING AROUND

Most of the historic sites, restaurants, and shops are walkable from the visitors center, so ditch your car in the public parking lot there ($3 per day) and proceed on foot.

▪▪▪▪ WHERE TO STAY

Galena is batty for B&Bs, with around 45 quilt-laden properties in the region. Most cost between $100 and $200 nightly, and they fill up on weekends. The visitors center (815-777-4390, 877-464-2536; www.galena.org) can tell you which ones have availability; the Web site provides contact info and descriptions.

Ryan Mansion B&B (815-777-2750; www.ryanmansiongalena .com), 11373 US 20. Ryan has all the parlors, marble fireplaces, and winding staircases you'd expect in a Victorian country estate. The seven rooms each have plush bedding and a private bathroom. Breakfast is big and fabulous. The library stocks heaps of fascinating old tomes. It all adds up to an historic treat, located 2 miles northwest of town. Rooms cost $95–250.

DeSoto House Hotel (815-777-0090, 800-343-6562; www.desoto house.com), 230 South Main Street. Located right smack downtown, the DeSoto dates from 1855 and has old-fashioned rooms with wallpaper and bright carpet. Presidents Grant and Lincoln stayed here, though they wouldn't have taken advantage of the in-room wi-fi. Rooms and suites come in varying sizes and cost $128–200.

Grant Hills Motel (815-777-2116, 877-421-0924; www.grant hills.com), 9372 US 20. Glamorous it ain't, and the standard-issue motel rooms won't win any design awards. But Grant Hills is a winner among low-cost options, with particular kudos for the outdoor pool, horseshoe pitch, picnic tables, gas grills, and pet friendliness. It's located 1.5 miles east of town. Rooms cost $69/79/89 for one/two/three beds; pooches are $10 extra.

▪▪▪▪ CAMPING

Apple River Canyon State Park (815-745-3302, www.dnr.state.il .us), 8763 East Canyon Road, Apple River (26 miles east of Galena). Open Apr. 15 through Oct. 31. Many outdoor enthusiasts consider Apple River Canyon the best camping in the region, thanks to its 47 quiet, scenic, and relatively spread-out sites. There are no showers, just water hydrants and pit toilets. Camp-sites are offered on a first-come, first-served basis (no reservations accepted). The cost is a hard-to-beat $8 per night.

Mississippi Palisades State Park (815-273-2731, www.dnr .state.il.us), 16327A IL 84, Savanna (27 miles south of Galena). Open year-round. This popular park has loads of campsites—241 sites to be exact (110 are electric)—but they're jammed close together. Three shower/flush-toilet buildings serve the grounds. There are also three primitive camping spots that require a half-mile walk in. The park's convenience store provides necessities like firewood. Campsites are offered on a first-come, first-served basis (no reservations accepted). Obtain permits at the north entrance park office. Electric sites cost $20, while nonelectric sites cost $10 per night.

▰▰▰▰ EATING OUT

111 Main (815-777-8030; www.one elevenmain.com), 111 North Main Street. Open Sun. through Thurs. 11 AM—9 PM, Fri. and Sat. 11 AM—10 PM. This low-key restaurant transforms Midwest meat-and-potato favorites into something special by using locally sourced ingredients from the area's small farms. Carve into braised pork 'n beans, almond-crusted walleye, meatloaf, and gooey mac 'n cheese knowing you're supporting the little guy. Beers and wines likewise flow from small-batch regional producers. Lunch mains, $8—12; dinner mains, $13—24.

Fried Green Tomatoes (815-777-3938; www.friedgreen.com), 213 North Main Street. Open Mon. through Thurs. 5 PM—9 PM, Fri. through Sat. 3 PM—9 PM. The name sounds homey, but Fried Green Tomatoes is upscale dining, Italian style. Pastas, veal, chicken, and seafood options fill the plates, washed down by a robust wine list. The interior's brick columns and warm wood trim make for a casual-romantic atmosphere. Dinner mains, $20—35.

Railway Cafe (815-777-0047), 100 Bouthillier Street. Open Mon. through Fri. 7:30 AM—3 PM, Sat. 8 AM—3 PM, Sun. 9 AM—3 PM. It's a simple café with a simple menu of cold sandwiches (think chicken salad), soups, and salads. In addition to using organic ingredients, the place wins kudos for serving Intelligentsia coffee—a fine way to start the morning or accompany one of the café's sweet treats. It's located across the street from the visitors center. Sandwiches, $7—10.

Clark's Again (815-777-4407), 200 North Main Street. Open Sun. through Fri. 5 AM—1:30 PM, Sat. 5 AM—3 PM. Clark's is a traditional diner serving traditional breakfasts, from the crack of dawn right on through to closing time. So pull up a stool at the counter or grab a table, then prepare for the onslaught of eggs, thick-cut bacon, pancakes, home fries, and biscuits and gravy. Lunchtime sandwiches are available, too. Breakfasts, $4—7; sandwiches, $5—8.

Many Civil War—era manors hold B&Bs these days.

VFW Hall (815-777-1003), 100 South Main Street. Open afternoons and evenings daily. Actually, there's no eating, but there is drinking in this retro, no-frills bar. Sip cheap beers and watch TV alongside veterans of long-ago wars. And don't be shy: as the big sign out front says, the public is welcome.

▮▮▮▮ WHAT TO SEE AND DO

Outdoor activities: Make your first stop **Fever River Outfitters** (815-776-9425; www.feverriver outfitters.com), 525 South Main Street. It rents canoes, kayaks, bicycles, snowshoes, and ice skates. It also leads guided tours.

For example, two-hour kayak tours on the Mississippi River's backwaters cost $45 per person; bird-watching kayak tours costs $45; and "adventure" tours that incorporate a 7-mile kayak, 3-mile hike, and 10-mile bike ride cost $85. Equipment is included in all prices. Or you can head out on your own. Kayak rentals cost $26/45 per half/full day. Bike rentals cost $16/25 per half/full day. Fever River also stocks good maps for pastoral bike routes in outlying areas (about $1 each).

Hiking and biking: In town, hop on the flat, 3.5-mile **Galena River Trail** (815-777-9772; www .galenarivertrail.com), beside the visitors center parking lot. It's an old rail track that's been converted. You share it with cars for roughly the first mile, then it turns off so you have the limestone bluffs and wildflowers to yourself.

Scenic drives: For those who prefer car-powered excursions to human-powered ones, Galena has you covered with two lovely drives. **Blackjack Road** is a hilly, 16-mile ridge road that runs between Galena and Hanover, passing farms, cottonwood trees, cows, and horses en route. Take Fourth Street from downtown, which becomes Blackjack Road. Also, the **Stagecoach Trail** morphs from Field Street downtown. It's a 26-mile drive on a narrow, twisty road en route to Warren. And yes, it really was part of the old stagecoach route between Galena and Chicago.

Horseback riding: Saddle up at **Shenandoah Rider Center** (815-777-2373; www.shenandoah ridingcenter.com), 200 North Brodrecht Road (about 8 miles east of Galena). Two-hour trail rides cost $75 per person; lessons cost $65 per hour.

Foodie tours: Take a culinary tour of a local organic farm with **Learn Great Foods** (866-240-1650; www.learngreatfoods.com). Trips vary but can include bison and cattle ranches, artisanal cheesemakers, herb farms, and wineries in northwest Illinois and southern Wisconsin. Tours are followed by a hands-on cooking class and dinner using fresh-from-the-farm produce, plus recipes to take home. Check the schedule online for locations. The cost is $95 per person. Reservations required.

Blueberry picking: Fill a bucket or three at **Wooded Wonderland** (815-777-1223, 815-777-3426; www.woodedwonderland .com), 610 Devil's Ladder Road (7 miles east of Galena off US 20). Open sunrise to sunset daily. Mid-July through mid-August is the prime season, though the farm stays open until October

selling other produce, honey, and jams.

Ghost tours: Set out on the hokey but fun **Annie Wiggins Ghost Tour** (815-777-0336; www.anniewiggins.com), 1004 Park Avenue. Held Fri. and Sat. evenings May through Oct.; call for times and reservations. Black-clad, lamp-toting Annie takes you to eerie spots where Galena's unquiet souls dwell. The hour-long tours cost $10.

▪▪▪▪ HISTORIC SITES

Ulysses S. Grant Home (815-777-3310; www.granthome.com), 500 Bouthillier Street. Open Wed. through Sun. 9 AM–4:45 PM Apr. through Oct., reduced hours Nov. through Mar. Grant lived here after the Civil War, from 1865 until 1869, when he left for Washington to become the nation's 18th president. Interpreters in historic costumes provide tours. Outside, look for the statue of Mrs. Butterworth, er, first lady Julia Grant. Suggested donation is $4 for adults, $2 for children.

Belvedere Mansion (815-777-0747), 1008 Park Avenue. Open Sun. through Fri. 11 AM–4 PM, Sat. 11 AM–5 PM, from late May through Oct. The antiques that spill out of this manor include some of history's most famous window hangings. Remember the green drapes Scarlett O'Hara rips down and sews into a dress in *Gone with the Wind*? Belvedere's got 'em. Tours are $12 for adults, $6 for children.

▪▪▪▪ DON'T FORGET

Main Street is nice and flat, but it's a glute-burning climb to the streets beyond. Wear comfy shoes. And make sure your brakes are well oiled, as many of the B&Bs are also situated high atop Galena's hilly roads.

▪▪▪▪ SPECIAL EVENTS

Mid-April: President Grant's Grand Birthday Celebration (www.galenahistorymuseum.org).

Mid-May: Galena Triathlon/Duathlon (www.galena.org/triathlon).

Mid-June: Great Galena Balloon Race (www.greatgalenaballoon race.com).

▪▪▪▪ NEARBY

Apple River Canyon State Park (815-745-3302, www.dnr.state.il.us), 8763 East Canyon Road, Apple River (26 miles east of Galena). Winding, hilly roads lead to this park, best known for its camping, hiking, and fishing amid limestone bluffs, deep ravines, and the picturesque namesake river. The five hiking trails are each about 1.5 miles long (one way). The bluff-side Primrose Trail wins top marks. If

you can manage the hills, the roads between the park and Galena are pretty for biking.

Chestnut Mountain (815-777-1320, 800-397-1320; www.chestnut mtn.com), 8700 West Chestnut Road (10 miles south of Galena). You can ski and snowboard right to the foot of the Mississippi River. The resort has 19 trails, a 475-foot vertical drop, half-mile runs, nine lifts, and a 7-acre terrain park.

Mississippi Palisades State Park (815-273-2731, www.dnr.state.il.us), 16327A IL 84, Savanna (27 miles south of Galena). Hikers and rock climbers proclaim this park to be the most beautiful in Illinois, thanks to its Mississippi River–front real estate, thick pine forest, and big, bold palisades (a.k.a. limestone

You never know what you'll find in Galena's old shops.

cliffs). Nine trails traverse the park, with several leading up to the bluffs' crests and providing views. Pick up trail maps at the north entrance park office.

▮▮▮▮ RESOURCES

Galena Visitors Center (815-777-4390, 877-464-2536; www.galena .org), 101 Bouthillier Street. Open daily 9 AM–5 PM. Located in the old train depot, it stocks a whopping amount of useful maps and info, including the *Galena & Jo Daviess County Visitors Guide*.

Jo Daviess County Farm Bureau (815-858-2235). Call these folks to receive the *Jo Daviess County Home Grown Guide*, a free booklet listing area farmers' markets, farm stands, orchards, and vineyards. It's also available at the visitors center.

18 • STARVED ROCK'S MANY SEASONS

Starved Rock State Park provides a shocking jolt of nature amid the Illinois cornfields. There you are, driving along through the pancake-flat middle of the state, when whammo—it slaps you with 18 waterfall-filled canyons, each slicing through tree-covered, sandstone bluffs.

Throw in a bald eagle sanctuary, activities from river rafting to cross-country skiing, and a peaceful old timber-hewn lodge for evening drinks, and it's clear why this is Illinois' most popular state park throughout the year.

The name comes from a grisly Native American legend. It's said that the local Illiniwek tribe murdered Pontiac, chief of the Ottawa. To avenge his killing, the Ottawa and their allies the Potawatomi went to battle against the Illiniwek and eventually chased them up a 125-foot butte. The Illiniwek were trapped without food. If they came down, they'd be killed by the waiting tribes. So they chose to stay on the rock, where they ended up starving to death.

Today you can schlep up the namesake rock via a congested maze of wooden stairs and decks, but it's more fun to wander the park's other 13 miles of hiking trails. Several ascend to the top of ridges, offering great views of the Illinois River, which forms the park's northern boundary and provides its fishing, boating, and birding opportunities.

No matter what the season, the park draws big crowds. In winter, it's all about the bald eagles who flock to the Rock when their feeding grounds in Canada freeze up. This is a great time to visit if you don't mind the cold, as there's also cross-country skiing and hiking to the canyons' glistening ice falls. In spring, these melt into cascading waterfalls and make good hiking destinations. Summer adds camping, canoeing, and horseback riding to the mix. And fall packs the park with visitors eager to see the 2,800 acres of woodlands flame into bright red, orange, and gold.

If the crowds at Starved Rock get to be too much, head 2 miles down the road to Matthiessen State Park. It's smaller, but still provides plenty of cliffy scenery to hike through. It's also well known for cross-country skiing and equestrian trails.

Nearby is the Vermillion River, where you can whitewater raft through laid-back rapids and canyons. Cyclists can hop on the I&M Canal Trail, an old mule path converted to a 60-mile bike trail that runs through the area. You can get on or off the I&M in downtown Utica.

Speaking of which, this little 1,000-person town sits 1 mile north of Starved Rock and makes a good base for stocking up on supplies. Bait, booze, and ice cream shops line the main road, along with a handful of restaurants and taverns. For a full-on retreat, you can park yourself at the park, and sleep, eat, and drink there without ever having to venture beyond.

▪▪▪▪ GETTING THERE

Starved Rock is 95 miles southwest of Chicago. Take I-55 south out of downtown. After 40 miles or so, merge onto I-80 west (near Joliet). Stay on I-80 for 45 miles to Exit 81 (IL 178, Utica). Go south (left) 3 miles on IL 178 and follow the signs into Starved Rock. The trip takes one and a half to two hours.

▪▪▪▪ GETTING AROUND

You can park at the visitors center and then walk to all the trails from there (though note that some are up to 4 miles away). Or you can drive to many of the trailheads, and park in their small lots.

▪▪▪▪ WHERE TO STAY

Starved Rock Lodge (815-667-4211, 800-868-7625; www.starved rocklodge.com), located inside the park just beyond the visitors center. The Civilian Conservation Corps built this cool, rambling stone-and-log structure in the 1930s. It sits on a high bluff facing the Illinois River and offers 71 motel-like guest rooms. They're fine, but the surrounding cabins have more character (albeit thin walls for noise). Each cabin is sectioned into four individual guest rooms, each with its own entrance and bathroom. Half the cabin rooms also have a fireplace. All guests have access to the lodge's indoor pool, hot tub, and sauna. A restaurant, lounge, and café round out the offerings. Rooms book up well in advance of special event weekends (see page 152), and the cabins are at a premium throughout the year. There's a two-night minimum stay on weekends. Lodge rooms cost $80–165, cabins start around $125.

Landers House B&B (815-667-5170; www.landershouse.com), 115 East Church Street, Utica. This B&B, sitting a convenient half-block from Utica's main drag, offers nine accommodations, all with private bathrooms. The cottages top the hierarchy, each sporting a whirlpool, fireplace, and screened-in porch among their amenities. The themed (safari! teepee!) suites are next, offering spacious quarters. A couple of peaceful rooms are also available. The filling breakfasts might be blueberry blintz soufflés, eggs Florentine, or crab quesadillas. There's a two-night minimum stay on weekends. Rooms/suites/cottages cost $149/259/329.

Grizzly Jack's Grand Bear Resort (866-399-3866 www.grizzlyjacksresort.com), near Starved Rock's main entrance on IL 178, Utica. If the kiddies demand a water park, this is the place. The resort offers a variety of room styles (including bunk beds). Rates start around $119 on weekdays and go up fast from there.

Starved Rock Inn (815-667-4238; www.shopcattails.com), located at the intersection of IL 178 and IL 6. The eight boxlike rooms here are clean and tidy, but they're well below the quality of other options in town. Then

Striated rock formations comprise Starved Rock's 18 canyons.

again, the price is also well below the other options—just be aware you get what you pay for. The inn is affiliated with Starved Rock Lodge, so guests have access to the pool and facilities there. Rooms cost $70.

▆▆▆▆ CAMPING

Starved Rock State Park Campground (815-667-4726; www.dnr.state.il.us), 2570 East 950th Road. Open year-round. The park's 133 electric campsites are not particularly leafy, but that doesn't stop them from being popular. It's best to reserve in advance, which can only be done by mail (call or visit the Web site for the reservation form). Or you can show up and hope to get lucky: 30 campsites are offered on a first-come, first-served basis. Two shower/flush-toilet buildings serve the grounds, and there's a store that sells firewood, ice, and other supplies. Sites cost $25 per night, $35 for holiday weekend nights, plus a $5 reservation fee.

▌▌▌▌ EATING OUT

Starved Rock Lodge Restaurant (815-667-4227), located inside the park just beyond the visitors center. Open 8 AM—9 PM daily. The restaurant does a nice job of cooking up native dishes. Chicken, fish, pheasant, and buffalo make appearances at dinner. Traditional omelets, burgers, and sandwiches, including several vegetarian and healthy options, do the trick for breakfast and lunch. Sunday brunch draws massive crowds for the all-you-can-eat buffet; reservations are essential. For drinks, you can't beat the lodge's rustic Back Door Lounge, open from 11 AM—11 PM daily. In summer, there's live music on the veranda overlooking the river. Breakfast, $5—8; lunch sandwiches, $7.50—10; dinner mains, $17—24.

Duffy's Tavern (815-667-4324), 101 Mill Street, Utica. Open 10 AM—1 AM daily. After a hard day of hiking, biking, or boating, nothing soothes sore muscles like a finely poured Guinness, complete with a shamrock drawn in the foam. Duffy's is a classic, old-school Irish pub, and as at all the good ones, a nice selection of European and local brews flow from its taps. Burgers and pub grub emerge from the kitchen.

Nodding Onion (815-667-4990), 522 Clark Street, Utica. Open 11 AM—3 PM and 5 PM—8 PM Thurs. and Fri., 8 AM—3 PM and 5 PM—8 Sat., 8 AM—3 PM Sun. Fuel up on hearty omelets and homemade sausage gravy for breakfast. Wraps (say, turkey and smoked bacon, or tuna wasabi) and panini (say prosciutto and mozzarella) fill the plates at lunch. Breakfast, $4.50—6.50; lunch sandwiches $7—7.50.

Foothill Organics (815-667-4700), 131 East Church Street, Utica. Open 10:30 AM—6 PM, closed Tues. The hippie vibe wafts strongly at this little shop next to Landers House B&B. Pick up baked goods made by locals in the community kitchen, or small portions of fresh-from-the-farm produce. First-time visitors get a free homemade cookie.

▌▌▌▌ WHAT TO SEE AND DO

Hiking: Thirteen miles of trails crisscross the park. The **Starved Rock Trail**, right behind the visitors center, takes you up the namesake rock via a congested maze of wooden stairs and decks. It's a great view at the top—especially in winter, when you can often see bald eagles—but it's more fun to lose the crowds and opt for the trails beyond. Spring is the best time for seeing waterfalls, with the **French Canyon**, **LaSalle Canyon**, and **St. Louis Canyon** trails topping the list (St. Louis can be a little hard to follow—remember to always bear to the right when the trail forks). These become ice falls in winter, and all the more beautiful. The **Illinois Canyon Trail** is a remote, birdsong-filled winner, though it can be muddy and plagued with mosquitoes after rainy periods. The trails are all fairly easy, with the longest coming in under 5 miles. Pick up trail maps at the visitors center.

Canoeing: To set float on the Illinois River, stop by **Starved Rock Adventures** (815-434-9200), the red-and-white-building in the visitors center parking lot. Open 11:30 AM–3 PM weekdays, 10:30 AM–5 PM weekends, from May through Oct. Don't worry: you won't be paddling on the open river by all the barges, but rather in a 1-mile stretch by Plum Island. The cost is $25 per hour, including all safety equipment.

Fishing: Everyone from dread-locked Rasta men to ice-cream-smudged kids cast lines from shore into the Illinois River. Most come away with good-sized catches. Fishing licenses cost $13 and are available from the bait shops in downtown Utica. Starved Rock Adventures (see above) rents fishing boats if you prefer to angle on the water.

Bird-watching: Bald eagles are the park's avian rock stars. See them from December through March, when they hang out on Plum Island. The park offers trolley tours ($22–27) to view them in January and February; call the visitors center for times. Or just stand atop Starved Rock itself and you'll likely see a few.

Starved Rock's timber-hewn cabins make a cozy getaway for any season.

Many fisher-folks reel in hefty catches from shore.

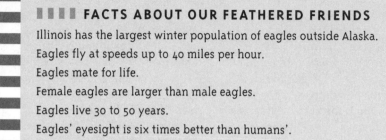

FACTS ABOUT OUR FEATHERED FRIENDS

Illinois has the largest winter population of eagles outside Alaska.

Eagles fly at speeds up to 40 miles per hour.

Eagles mate for life.

Female eagles are larger than male eagles.

Eagles live 30 to 50 years.

Eagles' eyesight is six times better than humans'.

The park is home to 200 additional bird species, including downy woodpeckers, blue jays, and red-tailed hawks. Pick up a complete list at the visitors center.

Horseback riding: Saddle up at **Starved Rock Horse Stables** (815-667-3026), on IL 71a half mile west of IL 178. Open Wed. through Sun., May 1 through Oct. 31. Guided rides leave at 10 AM, 12 PM, 2 PM, and 4 PM. The cost is $25 per hour.

River rafting: **Vermillion River Rafting** (815-667-5242; www.vermillionriverrafting.com), 781 North 2249th Road, Oglesby (about 5 miles south of Utica via IL 178). Departures at 9 AM and 2 PM daily, from May through mid-July (or later into the summer if there have been heavy rains). Plunge into easy, breezy Class 1 and 2 rapids on this four-hour, self-guided trip on the Vermillion River, where mighty canyons rise up alongside the water. The cost is $25 for adults, $20 for children under 16.

Biking: The **Illinois & Michigan (I&M) Canal Trail** rolls through downtown Utica. A 19th-century path where mules once towed boats along the waterway, it's now a crushed-stone bike trail spanning 60 miles between Channahon to the east and LaSalle to the west. Note that some portions remain closed due to flooding, including the bit between Utica and Buffalo Rock State Park, and riders must divert to local roads. For bike rentals, try **Mix's Trading Post** (815-667-4120), on IL 178 in downtown Utica. Open 9 AM–5 PM daily. Rentals cost $7 per hour, $20 per day.

DON'T FORGET

It's always handy to have plastic bags in which to isolate muddy shoes. Bring mosquito repellent in summer.

▪▪▪▪ SPECIAL EVENTS

Contact the lodge (800-868-7625; www.starvedrocklodge.com) for more information on these and other events:

Mid-January: Winter Wilderness Weekend.

Late January: Eagle Watch Weekend.

Early May: Annual Wildflower Pilgrimage.

Mid-October: Fall Colors Weekend.

▪▪▪▪ NEARBY

Matthiessen State Park (815-667-4868; www.dnr.state.il.us), on IL 178, 2 miles south of Starved Rock. If the crowds at Starved Rock are too much, try Matthiessen, which also offers dramatic cliffs and chasms formed by water runoff to the river. The park has 5 miles of hiking trails. They're primo for cross-country skiing in winter, when you can rent equipment from the trailer (815-664-2484) near the Dells Area entrance. Thirteen miles of equestrian trails also meander through the park. Note that Matthiessen has no park office or camping facilities.

▪▪▪▪ RESOURCES

Starved Rock Visitors Center (815-667-4906; www.dnr.state.il.us) Open 9 AM—4 PM daily. Pick up trail maps and birding and wildflower sheets.

19 • PEACE IN THE ROCK RIVER VALLEY

Sit. Smell the pines. Watch the clouds roll by.

If this sounds like your recipe for a relaxing getaway, then the Rock River Valley a few hours due west of Chicago is your place. In particular, White Pines Forest State Park is your spot, thanks to its sweet log cabins tucked far in the woods. Built by the Civilian Conservation Corps in the 1930s, they're ideal escapes where your biggest decision is when to stop counting shooting stars each night.

Two other low-key state parks are in the area, both abutting the Rock River as it surges east toward the Mississippi's waters. Castle Rock is known for canoeing and hiking, while Lowden (rhymes with *cow*-den) sports the hulking, 50-foot Black Hawk sculpture from its banks (remnants of an artists' colony). Sadly, as this book was going to press, the state government announced it might close the two parks due to budget cutbacks. Call before planning your visit. The small towns of Oregon and Dixon flank the parks.

Speaking of Black Hawk, chief of the Sauk, he was the main man around here until 1832. That's when clashes between the newly arrived settlers and long-standing native tribes erupted into violence, and the Black Hawk War drove the natives out.

A couple of presidents and the world's most famous tractor man also hung out in the valley. Young Abe Lincoln served in the local militia during the Black Hawk War; a statue in downtown Dixon marks the spot. Almost a century later, Ronald Reagan grew up in Dixon; hear all about it at his historic home. And then there's John Deere. He put down stakes a little farther upstream, where he invented the steel-blade plow and forever changed the local landscape. A still-operating blacksmith shop carries on his legacy.

The parks are open year-round. Summer is prime time, though White Pines' cabins are busy throughout the seasons. Visitors planning to camp or boat should call ahead—not only to check on the status of Castle Rock and

Lowden parks, but because Rock River flooding can wash out plans in a hurry.

As you drive around, keep an eye on the roadside for farms offering fresh produce and eggs for sale. Stopping to pick up a dozen is about as wild as it's going to get in this gentle valley.

■■■■ GETTING THERE

White Pines is 115 miles west of Chicago. From downtown, take I-290 west for 13 miles, and then merge onto I-88 west, a.k.a. the Ronald Reagan Memorial Tollway. Stay on the toll road for 86 miles. Exit at Dixon, and merge onto IL 26 north for a few miles. Turn right at IL 38/Lowell Park Road and stay on it for 9 miles. Turn right onto Pines Road. The park entrance is about 1 mile west. The trip takes two to two and a half hours.

■■■■ GETTING AROUND

From Oregon, Castle Rock is 3 miles away, Lowden is 2 miles, and White Pines is 10 miles. From Dixon, the parks are 12 miles, 18 miles, and 11 miles away, respectively.

■■■■ WHERE TO STAY

White Pines Inn (815-946-3817; www.whitepinesinn.com), 6712 West Pines Road, Mt. Morris. Open early March through late December. These little cabins in the big woods are the main reason to trek to the Rock River Valley. The one-room, stone-and-timber structures make you feel like Laura Ingalls—if Laura had a mini-fridge, gas fireplace, heating, air-conditioning, TV, DVD player, and shower in her pad. The queen-size, hand-hewn log beds are comfy. A double trundle bed tucks underneath, so the room can sleep four people total

White Pines' little cabins in the big woods give guests that pioneer feeling.

A blacksmith at the John Deere Historic Site fires up the anvil.

(though it's tight quarters). Best yet, each cabin is equipped with Adirondack chairs out front—a perfect place to sit back, smell the pines, and see the stars. A couple of community fire pits provide roasting opportunities. And you can read your cabin's journal to know the thoughts of those who've come before.

Because of all this rustic awesomeness, the 13 cabins are extremely popular. Advance reservations are essential in all seasons. There's a two-night minimum stay on weekends. Ask about deals during midweek visits. The cabins cost $94 per night.

Pine Creek Cabins (815-946-2236; www.whitepinesinn.com), 6559 West Pines Road, Mt. Morris. Open year-round. Run by the White Pines Inn folks and located just outside the park, these three larger cabins are designed for groups. Whispering Pine sleeps six or seven people. Knotty Pine and Porcupine sleep 12 people each. The cabins cost $174–214.

▪▪▪▪ CAMPING

Lowden State Park (815-732-6828), 1411 North River Road, Oregon. Open year-round (but call ahead, since the park might end up the victim of budget cutbacks). Lowden is the area's winner for camping, with 118 sites (80 electric and 38 nonelectric)

well-spread across quiet, green grounds by the Rock River. Showers, flush toilets, and a snack bar (in summer) serve the troops. A couple primitive walk-in sites enable hardcore tenters to get off the beaten path. All sites are offered on a first-come, first-served basis (no reservations), but securing a spot isn't a problem aside from holiday weekends. Primitive/nonelectric sites cost $6/10, electric sites cost $20 ($30 on holidays).

White Pines Forest State Park (815-946-3717; www.dnr.state.il .us), 6712 West Pines Road, Mt. Morris. Open year-round. Be sure and call before arrival, as the campground sometimes closes from flooding. The grounds have shower buildings and flush toilets, but the 103 sites do not have electricity. Noise from passing trains can be an issue. Sites are offered on a first-come, first-served basis (no reservations), and cost $10 per night.

Castle Rock State Park (815-732-7329; www.dnr.state.il.us), 1365 West Castle Road, Oregon. Castle Rock has a primitive canoe camping area only. Call ahead to see if it's open, since the park might end up the victim of budget cutbacks (or flooding, which occurs frequently). The eight campsites are a half-mile paddle from the boat ramp; you can leave your car in the ramp's lot overnight. The grounds have a portable toilet and fire pits. Campsites cost $6 per night.

▮▮▮▮ EATING OUT

White Pines Inn (815-946-3817), 6712 West Pines Road, Mt. Morris. Open Mon. through Thurs. 8 AM–8 PM, Fri. and Sat. 8 AM–9 PM, Sun. 8 AM–7 PM. The lodge whips up a decent meal any time of the day in its small, rustic dining room. There's oatmeal, egg-filled skillets, and biscuits and gravy in the morning; chicken potpie, veggie lasagna, and pork sandwiches in the afternoon; and meatloaf, salmon, and pasta in the evening. Quaff drinks in the attached Moose Lounge. Breakfast, $4.50–8.50; lunch mains, $6.50–8.50, dinner mains, $13–18.

Touch of Thai (815-284-8499), 221 West First Street, Dixon. Open Sun. through Thurs. 11 AM–9 PM, Fri. and Sat. 11 AM–10 PM. It's rare to hear words like edamame, tofu, and panang curry spoken in this part of the state, so take advantage of the refuge while you can. Mains, $7–8.

M&M Supermart (815-732-7427), 1000 Pines Road, Oregon. Open 7 AM–9 PM daily. Stock up on groceries and alcohol at this full-service supermarket.

▮▮▮▮ WHAT TO SEE AND DO

White Pines Forest State Park (815-946-3817; www.dnr.state.il.us), 6712 West Pines Road, Mt.Morris. The cabins (see Where to Stay, page 155) may be the park's crowning glory, but don't overlook the hiking trails. The seven paths total about 4.5 miles and provide short jaunts past limestone bluffs, wildflower jumbles, and of course, stately pine trees. The park grooms some trails for cross-country skiing in winter. If you prefer indoors to outdoors, look into the lodge's long-standing Dinner Theater, where you might catch a comedy revue or Neil Diamond tribute show.

Castle Rock State Park (815-732-7329; www.dnr.state.il.us), 1365 West Castle Road, Oregon. Quiet Castle Rock is a relaxed park for hiking, boating, canoeing, and picnicking. Seven miles of trails wind through woods and prairie. Anglers have 1.5 miles of riverbank to cast for catfish, bass, and walleye. There's also a public boat ramp. The park spreads over a sizeable chunk of land and has both north and south entrances. The north one is where most facilities are, including the boat ramp and park office. Before planning your visit, call to make sure the park is open, since it might end

up the victim of budget cutbacks.

Lowden State Park (815-732-
6828; www.dnr.state.il.us), 1411
North River Road, Oregon. The
big deal at this park is the Black
Hawk Statue—a 50-foot concrete
colossus that stands atop a cliff
and gazes down the Rock River.
Lorado Taft designed the 100-ton
sculpture as a tribute to all Native
Americans, but it's usually asso-
ciated with Chief Black Hawk
(though it doesn't bear his like-
ness). Taft—well-known for his
huge public sculptures in Chicago at the Art Institute and Washington Park—was part of the
Eagle's Nest Artist Colony in the
1920s, which set up by the Rock
River each summer to escape
Chicago's heat. A short drive
through the park takes you to the
mondo statue. Lowden also has
good facilities for camping,
boating, and fishing, and 4 miles
of hiking trails. Before planning
your visit, call to make sure the
park is open, since it might end
up the victim of budget cutbacks.

T.J.'s Bait, Tackle, and Canoes
(815-732-4516; www.tjscanoe
rental.com), 305 South First
Street, Oregon (on the riverbank,
two blocks south of the IL 64
bridge). Open weekends only 9
AM—2 PM Apr. through Nov. Rent a
canoe or kayak to launch from

T.J.'s site, paddle down the Rock
River, and then the company will
shuttle you back from either Castle Rock (a two-hour trip) or
Grand Detour (a four-hour trip).
Advance reservations required.
The cost is $32 per vessel for the
short trip, $47 for the longer trip,
life jackets included.

White Pines Ranch (815-732-
7923; www.whitepinesranch
.com), 3581 West Pines Road.
Located a few miles from White
Pines State Park (though not affiliated), this is a dude ranch for
kids. Drop off the tykes for one
week, two weeks, or the entire
summer for their fill of horseback
riding, swimming, campfires,
bunk-bed dorms, and mess-hall
eats. The cost is $525 per week,
all-inclusive.

▌▌▌▌ HISTORIC SITES

Ronald Reagan's Boyhood Home
(815-288-5176; www.ronaldreagan
home.com), 816 South Hennepin
Street. Open Mon. through Sat. 10
AM—4 PM, Sun. 1 PM—4 PM Apr.
through Oct., weekends only in
Mar., closed Nov. through Feb.
The United States' 40th president
lived in this good-size house
from 1920 to 1923. It contains no
original furnishings, though Reagan himself chose the reproduc-
tion decor from an old Sears cat-
alog based on his recollections of
the interior. Admission includes a

guided tour and 9-minute video. It's overkill unless you're a true-blue Reagan fan. Instead, ask the lively senior citizen volunteers who run the place if you can pop into the gift shop. Or gander at the bizarre statue in the yard where Reagan is admiring corn kernels in his hand. Admission costs $5.

John Deere Historic Site (815-652-4551; www.johndeerehistoric site.com), 8393 South Main Street, Grand Detour (6 miles northeast of Dixon on IL 38). Open 9 AM—5 PM daily Apr. through Oct. This was tractor man John Deere's home before he hit the big time and moved to Moline (where the company headquarters are today; see chapter 15 for details). Deere was originally a blacksmith who forged horseshoes, and he had his shop here in the 1830s. He kept hearing farmers complain that the cast-iron plows they brought with them from the East didn't work in the Midwest's gummy soil—dirt stuck to the blades, and farmers had to stop every few feet to clean them. Deere gave it some thought, then created a new plow with a modified shape and polished steel blade. Voilà—the dirt slid off. By 1837 his steel plows were all the rage, and his blacksmith shop became a plow factory. Eventually he moved to Moline to take

Lorado Taft's 50-foot Black Hawk statue stands sentry on the Rock River's banks.

advantage of better transportation along the Mississippi River.

The coolest thing about the site today is the still-operational blacksmith's shop. A big, sassy, gray-ponytailed gent named Rick fires up the anvil and forges metal artworks while you watch. There's also an extensive guided tour of the house. Admission is $3.

▪▪▪▪ DON'T FORGET

Bring your favorite DVDs for the cabins. Stock up on bug spray in summer.

▪▪▪▪ SPECIAL EVENTS

Mid-August: Reagan Trail Days (www.reagantraildays.net), Dixon. To honor the 40th prez, there's a Jelly Belly eating contest, horse parade, and—oddly—Thai music and kickboxing.

Late September: Scarecrow Festival (www.dixonil.com), Dixon. Pumpkin decorating, beanbag tournaments, and a whole lotta scarecrows invade main street.

Early October: Autumn on Parade (www.autumnonparade .org), Oregon. Tractors, quilts, and cider doughnuts rule downtown the first weekend of the month.

■ ■ ■ ■ RESOURCES

Blackhawk Waterway Convention and Visitors Bureau (800-678-2108; www.bwcvb.com) A good, overarching information source for the area.

20 • GENTEEL LAKE GENEVA

Old-money Chicagoans with names like Wrigley, Driehaus, and Drake have long summered in Lake Geneva. It was just a short train ride over the Wisconsin border to reach the shimmering sapphire water in the late 1800s, so wealthy families—sick of Chicago's crowds and heat—sped north and built pillared mansions along the waterfront, each one more elaborate than the next.

The deep blue water and proximity to the city keep Lake Geneva high on the getaway list today. And while the manor-strewn shoreline is sometimes called "the Hamptons of the Midwest," visitors of more modest means are just as welcome. Nowhere is this more evident than on the Lake Shore Path, the 21-mile public trail that goes through all water's-edge properties, from the smallest cottage right on up to the Wrigley estate. Other favorite pastimes here include riding on the mail boat, stargazing at the observatory, and antique hunting.

Let's clear up a technical matter before going any farther. "Lake Geneva" is the name of the lakeside town, while "Geneva Lake" is the name of the body of water. So Lake Geneva (population 7,100) sits at the edge of Geneva Lake. Williams Bay and Fontana are the two other towns on the lake's shore. They're smaller and more mellow than Lake Geneva, which bustles with restaurants, gift shops, realty companies, and chains like Starbucks, Cold Stone Creamery, and Anne Klein.

Delavan Lake and Lake Como are the area's smaller but equally busy watering holes, a quick hop to the north. Antique hounds should empty their car trunk before hitting the town of Delavan (population 8,000), where several shops cluster on Walworth Avenue, the old-fashioned, mom-and-pop main drag. Antiques also weigh down shelves in Elkhorn, a few miles farther north. If you're in town during its Sunday flea market, you might want to add a trailer to the car.

Summer is boom time at the lakes, when everyone splashes around in the beloved water. Geneva Lake, by the way, gets its true-blue hue from two things: its depth, which at 135 feet makes it Wisconsin's second-deepest lake; and the underwater springs that feed it, keeping water quality pure. Spring and fall still see vacationers, but winter is a quiet time in the area.

■■■■ GETTING THERE

Lake Geneva is about 80 miles northwest of Chicago. Take I-94 north to WI 50 west; the latter runs straight into town. Tolls cost $2.50, and roads can get crowded on weekends. The trip takes about an hour and a half to two hours.

■■■■ GETTING AROUND

WI 50 is the main vein connecting Lake Geneva and Delavan. It's a 10- to 15-minute drive between the two towns.

In Lake Geneva, the public parking lots are metered and monitored closely in summer. Bring lots of quarters.

■■■■ WHERE TO STAY

Most lodgings have a two-night minimum stay on weekends. Prices drop considerably in winter.

French Country Inn (262-245-5220; www.frenchcountryinn .com) W4190 West End Road (about 3.5 miles west of Lake Geneva via WI 50). Pretty little Lake Como laps the shore under this peaceful, romantic inn. Most of the 34 rooms have skylights or cathedral ceilings, a fireplace, and French doors that lead out onto a lakeside balcony. A separate building holds "luxury rooms," which add more space and whirlpools to the mix. A popular restaurant called Kirsch's is on-site for when hunger and/or thirst strike. There's an outdoor pool, and wireless access in the lobby only. Standard rooms including breakfast cost $155–165 on weekdays, $175–195 on weekends; luxury rooms start at $215.

WatersEdge B&B (262-245-9845; www.watersedgebb.com), W4232 West End Road (about 3.5 miles west of Lake Geneva via WI 50). This antique-laden, seven-room B&B fronts Lake Como and was where gangster Bugs Moran used to hang out. You can actually stay in the room where he counted his cash—ask for the Bugs Suite, accessed through a secret passageway. The rooms come in varying configurations, i.e., some have kitchen facilities, some have decks, some are suites with multiple beds. All have private bathrooms. The B&B is a few doors down from French Country Inn (see above). Rooms including breakfast cost $135–200 on weekdays, $150–235 on weekends.

Eleven Gables Inn (262-248-8393; www.lkgeneva.com), 493 Wrigley Drive (in downtown Lake

Geneva). This 1847 building was the first B&B on Geneva Lake, and it's a stone's throw from downtown's restaurants, shops, and the Riviera Docks. The six frilly rooms have private bathrooms and wireless Internet access; three of the rooms (Verandah, Wicker Courtyard, and Peach) have their own private entrance. For those who require air-conditioning, note that the Verandah and Rose rooms have fans only. Dogs are welcome with advance notice. Rooms including breakfast start at $169.

Grand Geneva Resort (800-558-3417; www.grandgeneva .com), 7036 Grand Geneva Way (a few miles east of Lake Geneva on WI 50). Hugh Hefner went way over the top when he built this place as a Playboy Club in 1968. You may still see bunnies today, but they'll likely be the small furry kind hopping through the resort's 13,000 acres. It's a crazy-huge spread that holds two golf courses, a ski and snowboard park, indoor and outdoor tennis courts and swimming pools, a spa, and hiking and biking paths. The 355 rooms sport dark, handsome decor and have balconies. Alas, the resort is not walkable to Geneva Lake, but it's doubtful you'll be leaving the grounds anyway. Rooms start at $229, plus a $12 resort fee.

▪▪▪▪ CAMPING

Big Foot Beach State Park (262-248-2528; www.dnr.state.wi.us /org/land/parks), 1550 South Lake Shore Drive, Lake Geneva (2 miles south of town). Open mid-Mar. through late Oct. The park's 100 campsites spread across grassy grounds shaded by oak trees. Facilities include hot showers, pit toilets, firewood for sale, and access to a beach on Lake Geneva (about a 10-minute walk away). Park entry by car requires a vehicle permit, which costs $10/35 per day/year. Reservations (888-947-2757; www.reserveamerica.com) are accepted for a $10 fee. Campsites cost $14.

▪▪▪▪ EATING OUT

It can be tough to find a good, nonoverpriced meal in the area, but options do exist. For instance,

The municipal pier at Williams Bay

you can nosh burritos and gua-camole in Delavan, where Walworth Avenue (the main street) holds several no-frills Mexican restaurants. Or join the locals for a lobster boil, pig roast, or pancake breakfast—community groups sponsor such events throughout the summer and fall, and they're open to the public. Check the chamber of commerce Web sites (see Resources, page 169) for listings.

Shrimp House (262-740-1335), 5576 WI 50, Delavan (behind the Dairy Queen in the strip mall). Open Wed. and Thurs. 11 AM—8 PM, Fri. 11 AM—9 PM, Sat. 11 AM—8 PM, Sun. 11 AM—7 PM. Great seafood from a highway-side strip mall in Wisconsin? Shrimp House delivers the goods. Its extensive menu spans everything from the namesake crustacean breaded and primed for cocktail sauce dipping, to oysters, fish tacos, Maryland crab cakes, and grilled trout. Sweet potato fries and hush puppies rank high on the side dish list. Eat in at the scattering of small tables, or get the food to go. The restaurant sits between Lake Geneva and Delavan. Grilled fish dinners, $7—10; one pound of breaded wild Gulf shrimp, $19.95.

Riga-Tony's (262-740-2540), 5676 WI 50, Delavan (in the strip mall by Shrimp House, above). Open Wed. through Sat. 10 AM—7 PM, Sun. 10 AM—4 PM. What happens when a couple of south-side Chicago restaurateurs are talked into retiring to Lake Geneva by their wives and get bored out of their skulls not long thereafter? They open a boisterous, home-style Italian eatery on the spot. The guys cook up different dishes daily—maybe spinach ravioli, maybe rice balls, maybe meatballs—for the small eat-in area. They also have a market/deli with baked goods, delicious fresh meats and cheeses, and all the requisite Italian condiments. Mains, $6—14.

Gilbert's (262-248-6680; www.gilbertsrestaurant.com), 327 Wrigley Drive, Lake Geneva. Open Tues. through Fri. 5 PM—9 PM, Sat. 5 PM—10 PM, Sun. 4 PM—8 PM. You know you're in for an upscale experience the moment you open the heavy doors and step into the elegant Victorian mansion. Gilbert's is serious fine dining, where eating can take up the better part of the night ("there's no rush on a good meal," as staff likes to point out). Dishes are local-meets-Pacific-Rim, like Amish-farmed chicken or pan-seared Alaskan halibut, and everything is organic. Order à la carte, or try the four- or six-course tasting menu (vegetarian version available). Certain nights have low-price specials if you eat before 5:30 PM. For instance, Wed. is half-price wine night, while Fri. is "date night" (i.e., three-course dinner for two for $50). Four-course menu, $60 per person; six-course menu, $75 per person.

▪▪▪▪ WHAT TO SEE AND DO

Walking and hiking: The 21-mile **Lake Shore Path** marches right around Geneva Lake—and right through mansion owners' front lawns. This wonderfully unique setup is a remnant of an old Native American treaty. In the 1800s, the local Potawatomi Indians under Chief Big Foot brokered an agreement with the white settlers to maintain the right to hunt and fish around the lake using their age-old path. The public's right to the trail remains today (it's a recognized public easement by federal case law), and landowners must leave it open to walkers.

You can hike the whole thing in a day, but the majority of people just walk a portion. The most historic section, with plenty of manors and bendy willow trees, runs between Lake Geneva and Williams Bay. It's about 6.5 miles (one way), flat, and without access once you set out, so you either keep going or turn back to get off the path. Williams Bay to Fontana is another good stretch. It's 1.75 miles (one way), again mostly flat, and meanders past mansions, summer camps, and the Yerkes Observatory. Public access points are few and far between. The main ones are at Lake Geneva (enter from the west end of Library Park), Williams Bay (enter from Edgewater Park) and Fontana (near the Abbey Resort, metered parking at the lakefront). Note that other portions of the path can be mountain-goat rugged.

If you don't want to retrace

A footbridge on the Lake Shore Path

Visitors can stargaze at Yerkes Observatory, home of the world's largest refractor telescope.

your steps, call **Lakes Area Taxi** (262-248-4770) for a lift; one-way between Williams Bay and Lake Geneva costs roughly $30. Better yet, time your walk to arrive in Williams Bay or Fontana at the same time as the cruise boats (see Boat tours, below) and hitch a ride back to Lake Geneva with them for about $20.

You'll greatly enhance your jaunt if you have a good map. Try to get the pocket-size Lake Shore Path guide ($5), published by *At The Lake* magazine (262-245-1000; www.ntmediagroup.com). It divides the route into short walks between public access points and provides information on all the sights you'll see along the way. It also gives detailed directions on how to follow the path, which can be tricky as it flickers in and out of private yards. Clear Water Outdoor (see Outdoor Activities, below) also has maps for sale.

More trails meander through wetlands, woodlands, and prairies at 230-acre **Kishwauke-toe Wildlife Preserve** (www .kishwauketoe.org) in Williams Bay. Pick up trail maps at the entrance (across from the beach), or download them from the Web site.

Boat tours: Getting out on the water is a must, so make your first call **Lake Geneva Cruise Line** (262-248-6206, 800-558-5911; www.cruiselakegeneva.com), 812 Wrigley Drive, Lake Geneva. It runs all the tours around the lake in vintage boats that leave from the Rivieria Docks downtown. The coolest ride is the 2.5-hour U.S. Mailboat Tour. You'll travel aboard one of the nation's few remaining vessels that delivers mail to piers. The kicker is the boat never stops—it slows down, and the young postal employee jumps off, tucks the mail into the pier box, and then jumps back on the moving boat. Other options include the two-hour Full Lake Tour, which is a bit of a long haul. The first half is the most interesting part—and happens to be what the hour-long Geneva Bay Tour covers. For whatever cruise you choose, sit on the right side of the boat as they all circle the lake counterclockwise. Most tours run between May 1 and Oct. 31. Costs range from $20 to $27.

Biking: The **White River State Trail** spans 12 mostly flat miles along an old rail bed between the towns of Elkhorn and Burlington. Rent bikes at **Pedal and Cup** (262-249-1111; www.pedalandcup .com), 1722 Main Street, a few miles north of Lake Geneva in Springfield via WI 120. It's open daily in summer, Fri. through Sun. only in May, Sept., and early Oct. You can hop on the trail right by the shop. When you're finished, you can replenish with coffee, ice cream, or other snacks. Trail passes (available at the shop) cost $4 per day, $20 per year. Bike rentals cost $7 per hour, $21 per half day, $35 for a full day (including overnight).

Outdoor activities: Those wanting to kayak, canoe, or otherwise play outdoors should stop into **Clear Water Outdoor** (262-348-2420; www.clearwateroutdoor .com), 744 West Main Street, Lake Geneva. The shop rents and sells all types of gear and provides paddling instruction and guided tours. For example, a 4-hour intro to kayaking class costs $90 per person, while a 2½-hour guided yoga class/sunset paddle costs $30. Or you can head out on your own. Kayak/canoe rentals cost $50/60 per two hours, $65/75 per four hours. For hikers, this is an excellent place to pick up Lake Shore Path maps and ask any questions about local trails.

Beaches: Geneva Lake's beaches are at Fontana (the best one, with a playground), Lake Geneva by the Riviera Pier, Williams Bay east of Edgewater Park, and Big Foot Beach State Park (see Camping, page 163). Lifeguards patrol all of them, and all have a fee (about $2 per child, $5 per adult). Delavan Lake also has a beach at the corner of South Shore Drive and WI 50. There are no lifeguards; admission is $1.50 per person.

Stargazing: Learn the secrets of the sky at **Yerkes Observatory** (262-245-5555; http://astro .uchicago.edu/yerkes), 373 West Geneva Street, Williams Bay. The University of Chicago's Department of Astronomy and Astrophysics, which operates the facility, offers tours every Sat. at 10 AM, 11 AM, and 12 PM year-round. You'll see the 90-foot dome that houses the world's largest refractor telescope. About once per month the observatory also hosts a night-sky-gazing event led by one of the astronomers; call for the schedule. Suggested donation for the 45-minute tour is $5, night events cost $25 per person.

▌▌▌▌ SHOPPING

Bibliomaniacs (269-728-9933), 324 East Walworth Avenue, Delavan. Open Tues. through Fri. 11 AM–6 PM, Sat. 10 AM–5 PM, Sun. 11 AM–4 PM. This used/antique bookstore provides hours of browsing. It's the kind of place where you can pick up a writing quill, a V. C. Andrews paperback, old sheet music, and *The Rubaiyat* in one fell swoop, and then sit in the shop's old rocking chairs and couches to examine your treasures. Three large cats prowl the store, but heed the sign at the counter: "If you bring up their weight, don't be surprised if we comment about yours."

Remember When Antiques (262-718-8670), 313 East Walworth Avenue, Delavan. Open Mon. through Sat. 9:30 AM—5:30 PM, Sun. 11 AM—4 PM. The search is over: the Princess Leia cookie jar you've always wanted is right here—along with thousands of other cookie jar likenesses you never dreamed possible. Remember When is the Midwest's largest cookie jar store/museum! Other antiques also cram the heaving shelves, as they do at shops up and down Delavan's main drag.

River Valley Ranch (262-539-3555, 888-711-7476; www.shrooms kitchen.com), 39900 60th Street, Slades Corners (8 miles east of Lake Geneva on WI 50). Open daily 9 AM—7 PM. Look for the barn with the big polka-dotted mushroom painted on it, and yep, 'shrooms galore spill out of the place. The Rose family hand-harvests them at their nearby farm, then brings them here to sell. You can get portabella, shiitake, oyster, and wild fungi in season, plus 'shroomy products like portabella salsa, pickled mushrooms, and do-it-yourself growing kits. The shop also sells herbs, heirloom vegetables, and pumpkins in season.

Elkhorn Antique Flea Market (414-525-0820; www.nlpromotions llc.com), Walworth County Fair Grounds on WI 11 (9 miles north-west of Lake Geneva). This mondo market is held on four different Sundays during the summer, from 7 AM—4 PM, usually in mid-May, late June, mid-Aug., and late Sept. More than 500 dealers, from seasoned pros to those who've just emptied Aunt Gertrude's attic, offer swell pick-ins in furniture, glassware, pottery, dolls, and just about everything else. There's a particularly good selection of country-style antiques. Admission costs $4, parking is free.

▪▪▪▪ SPECIAL EVENTS

Check the chamber of commerce Web sites (see Resources, page 169) for concerts in the parks, pig roasts, and much more.

Mid-August: Venetian Festival (www.lakegenevajaycees.org). Five days of boats, beer, bratwursts, and fireworks.

Early October: Fat Tire Memorial Tour (www.fattirememorialtour .com). A 21.5-mile bicycle tour through Lake Geneva, Fontana, and Williams Bay.

Early February: Winterfest (www.lakegenevawi.com/winter fest). Four days of winter activities capped by the U.S. Snow Sculpting Championships.

▮▮▮▮ NEARBY

Kettle Moraine State Forest's Southern Unit (262-473-6427; www.dnr.state.wi.us/org/land /parks) begins near Whitewater Lake, 14 miles north of Delavan via County Road P. Outdoorsy types can go wild amid the 20,000 acres of glacial hills, kettles (a type of geologic pothole, left behind by a melting glacier), flower-strewn prairies, and pine trees. The area is renowned for its hiking, mountain biking, cross-country skiing, and horseback riding trails. The Whitewater Lake Campground also draws hardy souls to its 63 primitive sites ($14 per night), where there are pit toilets but no shower facilities. Park entry by car requires a vehicle permit, which costs $10/day or $35/year.

▮▮▮▮ RESOURCES

Geneva Lake West Chamber of Commerce (262-275-5102; www .genevalakewest.com). Provides excellent information for the west-side towns of Williams Bay, Fontana, and Walworth, especially regarding local events. See the Web site or request a free *Vacation Guide*.

Walworth County Chamber of Commerce (800-395-8687; www .visitwalworthcounty.com). Information source not only for the lake towns but also for the less-touristed inland towns.

Lake Geneva Area Convention and Visitors Bureau (800-345-1020; www.lakegenevawi.com). Provides information on the lake towns, with an emphasis on Lake Geneva.

At The Lake (262-245-1000; www.ntmediagroup.com). Quarterly magazine that also publishes the useful, pocket-size Lake Shore Path guide ($5).

APPENDIX: *Additional Resources*

▊▊▊▊ ILLINOIS

Illinois Bureau of Tourism (800-226-6632; www.enjoyillinois.com).

Illinois state park information (217-782-6752; www.dnr.state.il.us). State parks are free to visit. Campsites cost $6 to $35; some accept reservations for a $5 fee.

Illinois highway conditions (800-452-4368; www.gettingaroundillinois.com).

Chicago Transit Authority (312-836-7000; www.transitchicago.com).

Metra (312-322-6777; www.metrarail.com).

▊▊▊▊ INDIANA

Indiana Office of Tourism (888-365-6946; www.visitindiana.com).

Indiana state park information (800-622-4931; www.in.gov/dnr). Park entry costs $2 per day by foot or bicycle, $7 to $10 by vehicle for nonresidents. Annual entry permits cost $46. Campsites cost $6 to $38; reservations accepted (866-622-6746; www.indiana.reserveworld.com).

Indiana highway conditions (800-261-7623; www.in.gov/indot).

▊▊▊▊ MICHIGAN

Michigan Travel and Tourism (800-644-2489; www.michigan.org).

Michigan state park information (800-447-2757; www.michigandnr.com/parksandtrails). Park entry requires a vehicle permit (nonresidents $8/29 per day/year). Campsites cost $16 to $33; reservations accepted (800-447-2757; www.midnrreservations.com) for an $8 fee.

Michigan highway conditions (800-381-8477; www.michigan.gov/mdot).

▊▊▊▊ WISCONSIN

Wisconsin Department of Tourism (800-432-8747; www.travelwisconsin.com). Produces loads of free guides on subjects like birding, biking, golf, and rustic roads.

Wisconsin state park information (608-266-2181; www.dnr.state.wi.us/org/land/parks). Park entry requires a vehicle permit (nonresidents $10/35 per day/year). Campsites cost $14 to $22; reservations accepted (888-947-2757; www.reserveamerica.com) for a $10 fee.

Travel Green Wisconsin (608-280-0360; www.travelgreenwisconsin.com). Program certifies restaurants, lodgings, and attractions that meet state standards for being environmentally responsible.

Bicycle Federation of Wisconsin (608-251-4456; www.bfw.org). Produces detailed maps and event information for cyclists.

Wisconsin highway conditions (800-762-3947; www.dot.wisconsin.gov).